Celebrations
FROM THE
Heart

Celebrations FROM THE Heart

Copyright © 2014 by CECA Enterprises, LLC

Artwork by Nall Hollis
Front cover, 9, 55, 63, 83, 90, 193, 211,
Nall's Haviland Collection series plates are featured on
Celebrations from the Heart menus.
Other china patterns by Nall are used throughout the book in photographs.

Photographs by Stephen DeVries on pages:
Back cover, 4, 19, 20, 23, 25, 29, 32, 34, 36, 41, 42, 45, 47, 60, 73, 79, 87, 89, 91, 93, 94, 98, 105, 108, 126,
145, 146, 148, 150, 152, 152, 155, 156, 157, 158, 159, 161, 162, 163, 164, 165, 166, 167, 169, 185, 199, 200,
201, 202, 203, 205, 206, 207, 208, 209, 213, 214, 217, 218, 221, 222, 225, 227, 233

Photographs by Robert Evers on pages:
11, 101, 106, 107, 111, 112, 113, 114, 115, 116, 117, 119, 120, 122, 123, 125, 127, 128, 129, 131, 132,
133, 135, 136, 139, 141, 142, 143, 172, 176, 179, 180, 181, 182

Photographs by Vicki Popwell on pages:
137, 170, 175, 177, 183, 229

Food styling by: Julia Rutland

Personal snapshots from private collections.

This book is a collection of our favorite recipes, which are not necessarily all original recipes.

Published by

Favorite Recipes® Press

An imprint of

SOUTHWESTERN
Publishing Group®

P.O. Box 305142
Nashville, Tennessee 37230
1-800-358-0560

Project Manager: Sheila Thomas
Book Designer: Dit Rutland
Production Designer: Steve Newman

Library of Congress Control Number: 2014947959

ISBN: 978-0-87197-631-4

Printed in the United States of America
First Printing: 2014
15,000 copies

ACKNOWLEDGMENTS AND DEDICATION

Since children have been such a focus in my life, I would like to dedicate this book to my children and grandchildren, to your children and grandchildren, and to all the little children whose lives hold the promise of our future.

This book would not have been possible without the constant support of my executive assistant Amanda Layton, whose hard work and dedication strengthen me and make every day easier. And of course my sweet family who willingly shares my time and allows me to take time away from them to be with you. The eloquent words that grace this book would not have been so elegant without the guidance from my dear sister, Charlotte Bent.

Love you more,

Sis

Thank you, dear family, for the love, support, and good times you have given me — and the courage with which you have faced life under many adversities, always with smiles, laughter and hope for the future — you know — "Laughter is the best medicine" — "William Shakespeare" — You have always been in my kitchen and my heart.

My heartfelt thanks go to my friend, Margaret Minton. We would have been lost without her loyal support and wonderful clerical skills during the writing of this cookbook.

Merci! Merci!

Betty

Our sincere thanks and appreciation go to these two beautiful ladies; without you, this cookbook would not have been possible.

Amanda Layton (L), Margaret Minton (R)

TABLE OF CONTENTS

FOREWORD

Sister

Why should you buy this book?! Because you love to celebrate with your family and friends and you love to cook and to share your recipes with friends and loved ones? You love Nall's fabulous illustrations and recognize an art book when you see one? Or is it because you love a book that wraps you up in a warm, happy memory of your own family celebrations? Maybe you just like Betty, Nall, and Sister! If you're like me, the answer is, all of the above.

"Her name," Mama told me, "is Patricia." But being one year old and somewhat limited in vocabulary, I couldn't get it right...so Mama said, "Just call her Sister." And she has been "Sister" ever since! That's how I know Sister. I have loved her for her whole life, and it is my happy privilege to share my thoughts on her lovely new book. This is not a cooking compendium, but rather, a guide to preparing a memorable Southern-style family event, with tips for decorating, preparing, and serving, as well as suggestions for wines that pair well with the menus, and enjoying your role as host or hostess. Aside from Southern cooking and fine art, these three friends have another bond; they all sponsor charitable foundations. Your purchase helps each charity, and in return you receive their creative inspiration. I think it's something to celebrate!

Charlotte Wood Bent

Betty

I am the oldest of four children. My siblings, Sheri, Bill, and Lisa, and I have always been a close-knit group. Our Sims family adventure has been filled with happy times, family traditions, and early life lessons that tested our resilience. Looking at our family from the outside, you would never know that we have been faced with childhood and other cancer mysteries as well as our brother Bill's hopeless battle with ALS.

Mom is the matriarch, the pillar of strength for all of us. Betty Sims is not only the quintessential optimist and ultimate supermom, but she is known within our family and throughout the circles of our hometown of Decatur, Alabama, and beyond as the "Queen of Hospitality." This truly amazing woman, the kind who would do anything for her family, also thinks nothing about having 300 people over for dinner. For many years, Mom has shared her passion for cooking and entertaining through her cooking classes and Southern Scrumptious cookbooks, but now...she is embarking on an adventure with two dear friends.

Through their individual passions for good food, fine artwork, and generous hospitality, Betty, Sister, and Nall have a common thread and a southern spirit that bind them together. You are going to love the fruits of their collective labor and talent in *Celebrations from the Heart!*

Mom has kept a sense of humor through challenging times and adversity. She is able to kick up her heels... not only on the dance floor but in the kitchen, too. She thinks well on her feet and has always loved to laugh! She certainly knows how to make lemons into lemonade...and into lemon curd!

Libby Sims Patrick

SISTER AND BETTY'S
Road Trip

PROVENCE, FRANCE, OCTOBER 2012

Everything was growing—our friendship, requests for our shared cooking classes, opportunities to speak all over the south about our love of cooking, our common interest in spreading the word about the charities we are so passionate about. We didn't realize it, but it was all leading up to a major decision.

In the spring of 2012, we decided that in order to enhance our culinary education, a trip to France was in order. We enlisted our husbands, George and Bill, to share our grand adventure to Julia Child's château in Provence, where we spent a full week immersed in French culture and cooking. The countryside was breathtaking, the air fresh and clean, and the food—well, "amazing" doesn't begin to paint that picture.

The château owner, Cathy Alex, was a charming hostess. She took us shopping for the freshest ingredients at the local markets and shared her vast knowledge of local culture and gastronomy. We spent a full day in the home of a wonderful French chef who prepared a memorable duck dinner for us, true to his French style.

Much of our free time was spent visiting French bakeries searching for just the right blend of French flours for a new bâtarde (baguette) Sister was in the process of developing. We are pleased to report that we were successful and Sister Schubert's® Mini Baguettes are now available in your grocer's frozen bread case.

With our patient menfolk in tow, we journeyed on to Paris and the famed Le Cordon Bleu cooking school, where we enjoyed even more of our French culinary education.

Finally, the road led us to the village of Vence, France, and the lovely estate of Nall Hollis, world renowned artist, fellow Alabamian, Sister's cousin, and a longtime friend of the Sims family. He is known internationally simply as "Nall."

When the talk of writing a cookbook finally became more than just talk, it seemed only fitting that we include Nall in our endeavors. Several of his beautiful china patterns and art pieces are found gracing pages throughout the book, some of which Nall graciously created exclusively for *Celebrations from the Heart*.

Food and celebrations go hand-in-hand. Whether it is a weekly Sunday supper, a special occasion, a holiday brunch for family, or a romantic dinner for two, our menus focus on coming together, connecting, and sharing. Our hope is that you will soon be hosting your own *Celebrations from the Heart*!

Bon Appétit!

Sister and Betty

GREAT CHEFS

Two of the greatest chefs of all time and friends of Nall's cooked for the inauguration of the N.A.L.L. Art Association in Vence, France. Among the guests were HSH Prince Albert II of Monaco and Ringo Starr. Several years later, two of the South's most revered chefs, Frank Stitt and Chris Hastings of Birmingham, followed in the footsteps of these great chefs when they traveled to France to cook the food for the opening of Alabama Art in Vence.

ROGER VERGÉ
PORTRAIT, BY NALL
Chef Roger Vergé, whose restaurant, Le Moulin de Mougins, located in the hills of Cannes, a beautiful converted 16th-century oil mill, was just across the way from Picasso's home for many years. Vergé is considered one of the greatest chefs of his time. He is the pioneer of the nouvelle cuisine, one of the chefs in France who broke away from the rigid grip of traditional Provençal values.

ALAIN DUCASSÉ
PORTRAIT, BY NALL
Considered by many to be France's most famous chef, Alain Ducasse received his first three-star Michelin rating when he was just 33. He now has 12 restaurants in France and others in 6 different countries with a combined Michelin star count of 20. The author of many cookbooks, his most recent, *Cooking for Kids*, was released earlier this year.

COOKING IN PROVENCE:
Recipes from La Pitchoune

MENU

Egg Cups with Olive Tapenade

Warm Brie Cheese en Croûte
with Curly Endive and Walnut
Vinaigrette

Purée de
Pommes-de-Terre à L'Ail

Provençal Tomatoes

Suprême de Volaille en Croûte
de Champignons

Sister's Baguettes

Chocolate Pots de Crème

WINE SUGGESTIONS:
Bourgogne Blanc French Rosé

EGG CUPS WITH OLIVE TAPENADE

2   ripe tomatoes, peeled and finely chopped

Salt and pepper to taste

Olive oil

2   tablespoons mayonnaise

3   extra-large eggs, hard-cooked, peeled and finely chopped

Olive Tapenade

¼   cup sour cream or crème fraîche

Fresh herbs for garnish

Season chopped tomatoes with salt, pepper and olive oil to taste; set aside.

Add mayonnaise to chopped eggs and mix to combine; mixture should be just moistened. Using a teaspoon or pastry bag, place a small amount of Olive Tapenade in the bottom of each egg cup. Add a good-sized layer of tomatoes. Top with a layer of egg mixture.

Finally, spoon on a thin layer of sour cream. Decorate with a sprig of fresh parsley, thyme or chive.

Olive Tapenade

1   pound Niçoise olives, pitted

2   anchovy filets

1   garlic clove, chopped

2   tablespoons capers, drained

3   tablespoons olive oil

Freshly ground black pepper to taste

Place olives, anchovies, garlic and capers in bowl of food processor and process until puréed. Add olive oil in a slow stream while processing. Add pepper to taste.

Yield: 6 to 8 egg cups

NOTE: A pound of Kalamata olives, pitted, may be substituted for the Niçoise olives.

To serve as an appetizer as seen in the photograph at left, place the cheese in the center of the dough. Fold the dough up over the sides of the cheese, pleating the upper edges to fit snugly around the cheese. Pinch dough together in the center to seal. Brush the dough evenly with the egg wash and place on parchment-lined baking sheet.

Bake at 375 degrees until pastry is golden and crisp, 40-45 minutes. Let it rest for 5 minutes, then transfer to a platter along with a sharp knife. Serve with plain water crackers.

WARM BRIE CHEESE EN CROUTE WITH CURLY ENDIVE AND WALNUT VINAIGRETTE

You may prepare the Brie (chilled overnight) for Warm Brie with Walnut Vinaigrette the day before, and bake just prior to serving.

½ cup walnuts

1 (9-ounce) Brie round

4 sheets filo dough, thawed per package

1 egg, lightly beaten

1 cup peanut or vegetable oil

4 cups curly endive or baby greens, washed, dried and torn into bite-sized pieces

Walnut Vinaigrette (recipe follows)

Preheat oven to 350 degrees. Place walnuts on a baking sheet and bake for 10 minutes. Chop finely and set aside.

Cut Brie in ½×4-inch slices. Cut filo dough sheets in half, crosswise. Working with one sheet of dough, with the smaller edges at the bottom and top, place a piece of Brie about a half inch from the lower edge. Turn the bottom edge over the Brie and roll over two times. Turn the two edges over the Brie and brush with beaten egg on the upper two inches of filo. Continue folding, pressing the final edge to seal. Place on a parchment-lined baking sheet, seam side up. Cover with plastic wrap and chill until ready to fry.

To prepare, heat peanut oil in a medium saucepan over medium-high heat. Fry the Brie until filo is golden brown, turning to brown both sides. Place on paper towels to drain.

Toss the greens with Walnut Vinaigrette and mound on individual plates. Place a portion of Brie on each and sprinkle with chopped walnuts.

Walnut Vinaigrette

1 tablespoon mayonnaise

1 tablespoon Dijon mustard

2 tablespoons white wine vinegar

1 tablespoon olive oil

¼ cup walnut oil

Salt and freshly ground black pepper

Place mayonnaise and mustard in a small bowl and whisk to combine. Add vinegar and blend well. Add oils in a slow stream while whisking to incorporate. Season with salt and pepper to taste.

Yield: 4 salad servings

PUREE DE POMMES-DE-TERRES A L'AIL

Garlic Mashed Potatoes

Garlic Cream

¼ cup peeled garlic cloves
(about 8 large)

¼ cup heavy cream

Potato Purée

1 pound (about 4 medium) Russet
potatoes, peeled and quartered

6 tablespoons coarsely chopped
unsalted butter, softened

¼ cup heavy cream

Salt and freshly ground black pepper
to taste

For the Garlic Cream, place garlic in a heavy medium saucepan. Cover with three inches of cold water. Bring to a slow boil. Drain and rinse with cold water. Repeat the process two more times. Coarsely chop the garlic and return it to the same saucepan along with the cream. Bring to a boil, then reduce heat and simmer gently until reduced by half or to a thick, sauce-like consistency, stirring occasionally. This may be prepared ahead, covered and set aside at room temperature.

For the Potato Purée, place potatoes in a heavy medium pot. Cover with cold water, add salt and bring to a boil. Reduce heat and simmer until tender, about 20 minutes. Drain well. Place butter in a large bowl and, using a potato ricer or food mill, press potatoes over the butter.

Up to one hour before serving, add ¼ cup heavy cream to the Garlic Cream and reheat until warm, stirring occasionally. Mix the warm Garlic Cream into potato mixture in a slow stream. Season with salt and pepper. This can be prepared one hour ahead and kept warm over a larger pan of gently simmering water. Stir occasionally.

Serve immediately.

Yield: 4 servings

 BETTY'S Best! Garlic Mashed Potatoes are a favorite of ours, and although we were taught "the long way" to prepare them, we prefer to simmer the garlic in cream without all that rinsing.

PROVENCAL TOMATOES

6 medium tomatoes, ripe but firm

2 tablespoons olive oil

1 small onion, finely chopped

2 garlic cloves

Salt and freshly ground black pepper

1 tablespoon fresh thyme leaves

2 tablespoons fine dry bread
crumbs

3 tablespoons grated Parmesan

Wash and core tomatoes. Over medium heat in a skillet or ovenproof pan large enough to hold tomatoes, heat olive oil. Add onion and garlic and cook until softened, but not browned, about five minutes. Place tomatoes, stem end down, over the onion mixture; season with salt and pepper and sprinkle thyme leaves over the tomatoes. Reduce heat to low and cook 25 minutes or until tomatoes are soft and their juices have evaporated.

Preheat oven to 425 degrees. Turn tomatoes over and place close together in baking dish. Mix bread crumbs and Parmesan together and stuff the tomatoes. Drizzle with a small amount of additional olive oil. Bake for about 25 minutes or until bread crumbs are browned.

Yield: 6 servings

SUPREME DE VOLAILLE EN CROUTE DE CHAMPIGNONS

Tangy Chicken with Mushroom Crust

The Tangy Chicken with Mushroom Crust is a bit challenging to prepare, but we love it and it is worth your time for a special occasion.

Chicken

2   tablespoons olive oil

¾   pound button mushrooms, ends trimmed and sliced

¾   pound fresh wild mushrooms (cremini, shiitake, portobello), ends trimmed and sliced

2   large shallots, peeled and coarsely chopped

2   large garlic cloves, peeled and minced

Salt and freshly ground black pepper to taste

6   large chicken breasts, boned, skinned and trimmed; fillet and tendon removed and reserved

2   tablespoons fresh thyme or chives

2   tablespoons chilled unsalted butter, coarsely chopped

Tangy Sauce

For the mushrooms, place a heavy large skillet over medium-high heat and film with oil. Add mushrooms, shallots and garlic and cook until mushrooms are lightly browned, about five minutes, stirring occasionally. Cool completely, refrigerating if necessary. Season generously with salt and pepper.

For the crust, grind fillets in a food processor until a smooth paste occurs, pulsing on and off. Add mushroom mixture and fresh herbs; pulse to chop coarsely.

Line a large baking sheet with parchment. Pat chicken breasts dry and season with salt and pepper. Divide mushroom mixture into 6 portions.

Place a 12-inch length of plastic wrap on a work surface. Place one portion of the mushroom mixture in the center of the plastic. Fold wrap over the mushroom mixture. Pat to an even thickness, slightly larger than the chicken breast. Place the breast, smooth rounded side down, on top of the mushroom mixture. Gather plastic wrap tightly up and around the chicken breast as if wrapping a gift basket, until the mushroom mixture adheres to the top and sides of the chicken breast. This may be prepared ahead of time and refrigerated.

To serve, preheat oven to 350 degrees. Bake chicken for 10 to 12 minutes. Remove from the oven and tent loosely with foil; allow to rest 12 minutes. Slice breasts diagonally.

Reheat Tangy Sauce by stirring it over medium-high heat. Whisk in butter. Ladle a pool of sauce onto a serving plate and arrange sliced chicken breasts over the sauce, fanning the slices. Serve immediately.

Tangy Sauce

2   medium oranges

2   large shallots, peeled and coarsely chopped

1   cup dry white wine

1   cup balsamic vinegar

2   cups unsalted chicken broth

2   tablespoons tomato paste

Salt and freshly ground black pepper to taste

Remove zest of oranges, without any of the white pith, using a vegetable peeler. Chop the orange peel coarsely and place it in a heavy medium saucepan with shallots, white wine and vinegar. Boil over medium-high heat until reduced to ½ cup. Add chicken broth and tomato paste and boil until reduced to one cup. Strain the mixture through a fine sieve, pressing ingredients with the back of a spoon. Season with salt and pepper. This can be prepared ahead and set aside at room temperature for several hours or refrigerated overnight.

Yield: 6 servings

NOTE: The Tangy Sauce may be prepared a day in advance. The crust can be made and the chicken coated at any time during the day the dish is to be served. Cook the chicken and reheat the sauce immediately before presentation.

SISTER'S BAGUETTES

3 cups French-style flour

1 to 1 ¼ cups lukewarm water

2 teaspoons instant yeast

1 ½ teaspoons salt

4 tablespoons olive oil

1 tablespoon sugar

In a large bowl, stir together flour, 1 cup water, yeast, olive oil, sugar and salt until thoroughly mixed. Cover the bowl and let dough rest for 30 minutes.

Knead the dough for five to seven minutes, or until it is very smooth. This is easily done with an electric mixer, or in the bucket of a bread machine. Transfer the dough to a lightly greased bowl, cover and let rise at cool room temperature (about 70 degrees F) until doubled in bulk, about 1 ½ hours.

Transfer dough to a lightly greased work surface and divide it into three pieces. Stretch each piece into a 15- to 18-inch-long loaf. Place each in a lightly greased baguette pan, or on a lightly greased baking sheet. Tent the loaves with lightly greased plastic wrap, and let them rise until puffy, about one hour.

Preheat oven to 450 degrees. Spritz the loaves heavily with warm water, then put them into the hot oven and bake for 20 to 25 minutes, or until crusts are a deep, golden brown. Remove baguettes from the oven, slip them off the pan, and return them to the oven rack. Turn off oven and crack the door about an inch. Allow the bread to cool fully in the oven.

Enjoy them the same day they are made or re-warm, loosely wrapped in foil, in a preheated 350-degree oven for 6 to 10 minutes.

Yield: 3 baguettes

SISTER Says! If you are not familiar with French-style flour, here's a little background. It is milled from fine, hard white wheat and is high-ash and medium protein. If your real question is where to find it, specialized baking stores and online sites make it available to every would-be French chef!

Bill & Betty, Sister & George with Kathy Alex in Julia's kitchen at La Pitchoune. In the background is the famous pegboard that Paul, Julia's husband, put up for her with each utensil drawn on it so she knew where each utensil should be put back in place.

CHOCOLATE POTS DE CREME

2	cups heavy cream
2	cups half-and-half
⅔	cup sugar
⅔	cup bittersweet or semisweet chocolate chips
6	egg yolks
2	whole eggs
½	cup unsweetened cocoa powder

Salt

| 2 | teaspoons vanilla extract |

Whipped cream for garnish

Preheat oven to 325 degrees. Warm cream, half-and-half, sugar and chocolate in a 2-quart glass cup in the microwave for two minutes on high. Whisk and return to microwave two minutes more until steam rises and chocolate is melted.

Whisk yolks, eggs, cocoa and a pinch of salt together in a bowl. Add warm chocolate mixture in a slow stream, whisking constantly. Stir in vanilla and strain into a measuring cup with a pour spout. Spoon off any foam and discard. Divide mixture among six 3-ounce pot de crème molds or oven-safe ramekins. Cover each mold tightly with lid or foil. Arrange molds in a baking dish, being careful that molds do not touch each other or the sides of the baking dish. Transfer dish to the oven and carefully add hot water to baking dish so that it reaches about halfway up on the molds.

Bake 35 minutes, and then check for doneness. Custard should be just set but still quiver like gelatin. If necessary, bake another three to five minutes. When custards are set, remove them from water bath and cool for 30 minutes at room temperature. Chill until completely cold, preferably overnight. Garnish each with a dollop of whipped cream.

BETTY'S Best!

Continuing your education in French cuisine, you have now been introduced to a "bain marie," or water bath. The technique is designed to cook mousses, custards, sauces, and even cheesecake in a manner that will help prevent breaking or curdling. It is also a good way to "hold" prepared dishes, ensuring their perfect warmth when serving.

ENTERTAINING TIPS

- Set the table at least a day ahead so that you're free to cook or relax the day of the event.

- Prepare as many foods in advance as possible. You will be glad you got a head start, and flavors will be enhanced.

- Decorate with fresh flowers. Buy potted plants (amaryllis, paperwhites, and herbs) two weeks in advance and fresh flowers (tulips and hydrangeas) no more than two days before.

- Collect nice vases; they make up half of the look of the flower arrangements.

- Add flowers, branches, leaves, and berries from the garden.

- Take advantage of the colors and smells of the time of year to provide guests with a full sensory experience.

- For special holidays, candles can make a big statement for little cost. Pillars in glass cylinders are more cozy and versatile in ivory than in white.

- Mix different textures of the same color family in fabrics, flowers, and accessories for extra interest.

- Incorporate something handwritten, such as a menu or place cards on the table. If serving buffet-style, it's a nice touch to have the recipe name creatively displayed next to each dish.

- Make a playlist and choose music that will be entertaining and pleasant, not too loud.

- Make guests feel special by welcoming them with a refreshing drink and sending them home with something homemade from your kitchen.

- Invite friends you think will genuinely enjoy one another. Whether or not they've ever met.

- Written invitations are always preferable, but the telephone or online invitations are far more common today and perfectly acceptable.

- Invitations to a party should go out two to three weeks in advance; for a party on or near a major holiday, send invitations at least a month ahead of time.

WINE PAIRINGS FOR BEGINNERS

SPARKLING WINE:

Champagne	Cremante	American
Prosecco	Sparklers	
Cava	Lambrusco	

Sparkling wine goes with a great variety of dishes., more sothan any other wine. It goes with pizza, fried chicken, scrambled eggs, and most anything. Sparkling "rose" can even work with meaty main courses.

LIGHT, CITRUSY, LIGHT-BODIED WHITE WINE:

Pinot Grigio	Vinho Verde	Muscadet Albarino
Sauvignon Blanc	Gruner Veltliner	

These tangy unoaked wines wake up your taste buds and make your mouth water. They perk up dishes that otherwise seem bland. They are the only wines that already have great acidity such as a grapefruit salad. Always make sure that the wine is as tart as the food. Salmon goes great with a muscadet.

RIPE FULL-BODIED WINES:

Chardonnay	Viognier	Marsanne
Chenin Blanc	Roussanne	

Full-bodied white wines tend to come from warmer climates and spend time in oaks, which gives them weight and richness. They are tricky to pair with food, but when they work, they are terrific. Pair with roast, poultry, and meaty fish, and starchier things like pasta.

JUCIER MEDIUM-BODIED REDS:

Pinot Noir	Gamay	Mencia
Barbera	Sangiovese	

There is a reason so many people love pinot noir. It is fruity and bright. All these wines have a vibrant acidity that makes them extremely versatile with mushrooms, lighter meat dishes, and tomato-based recipes, such as rigatoni and lasagna.

STRUCTURED RICH FULL-BODIED REDS:

Cabernet Sauvignon	Malbec	Cabernet Franc
Bordeaux	Syrah	Merlot

Whatever their reputation, these rich lush wines all demand meat. Match the powerful reds with equally substantial dishes like braised short ribs or spicy grilled steaks.

SERVE RED WINE BETWEEN 50 and 64 degrees.

SERVE WHITE WINE BETWEEN 39 and 50 degrees.

THE AMERICAN FEAST!
Thanksgiving
DINNER

One of Sister's favorite holidays, Thanksgiving has always been a happy reunion of two large families blessed with many children. George and Sister have five children and seven grandchildren so far, and that's the core group. Add a few aunts, uncles, and cousins, and you have a party! The décor varies from year to year, but usually features fresh cut magnolia boughs, seasonal chrysanthemums, and bright crystal bowls of cranberries and oranges interspersed among silver epergnes and candles. Charlotte and Chrissie, Sister's daughters, collaborate on special decorations for the children's tables. The basic menu always contains a few comfortable family favorites, but Sister likes to add new recipes every year as well; who knows when a new family favorite will appear? With so many to feed, there are usually two big turkeys, one roasted and one smoked or deep fried, plus Old-Fashioned Cornbread Dressing with Gravy, Holiday Cranberry Salad, and Sweet Potato Orange Cups. Everyone loves the Pecan and Caramel Pies and of course Pumpkin Mousse. Not to mention heaping trays of Mam-mommy's rolls.

For the Sims family, Thanksgiving is everyone's favorite holiday and the family comes together from Atlanta, Nashville, and Florence. Dinner is always served in the formal dining room, where a large cornucopia filled with seasonal fruit and ribbon is the centerpiece. Each person tells what they are thankful for, and at the end of the dinner, a special candle is lit in memory of Bill Jr., their son, who died of ALS.

HOLIDAY CRANBERRY SALAD

MENU

Warm Spiced Cider

Holiday Cranberry Salad

Brined Turkey Roasted with
Rosemary and Thyme

Old-Fashioned Cornbread
Dressing with Great Gravy

Citrus Sunshine Sweet Potatoes

Confetti Roasted Vegetables

Spiced Cranberries

Sister's Original
Parker House Rolls

Pumpkin Mousse

Fabulous Caramel Pie
with Meringue

Pecan Pie

WINE SUGGESTIONS:

Pinot Gris and Pinot Noir,
preferably from Oregon's
Willamette Valley

WARM SPICED CIDER

8 cups apple cider

¼ cup sugar

1 medium orange, thinly sliced

1 lemon, thinly sliced

1 lime, thinly sliced

2 (3-inch) cinnamon sticks

12 whole allspice berries

8 whole cloves

Additional orange slices for garnish

Additional cinnamon sticks for garnish

Combine all ingredients in a 3-quart saucepan. Simmer over low heat, stirring occasionally, for 24 minutes. Do not boil. Strain mixture and discard solids.

Divide cider among eight serving mugs and garnish each with an orange slice and cinnamon stick, if desired.

Yield: 8 servings

HOLIDAY CRANBERRY SALAD

3 (3-ounce) packages black cherry-flavored gelatin

1 cup sugar

2 cups boiling water

1 (15.25-ounce) can crushed pineapple

2 tablespoons lemon juice

2 cups ground fresh cranberries

2 small seedless oranges, unpeeled, ground

2 cups finely chopped celery

1 cup chopped walnuts

Lettuce leaves

Sugar-Frosted Cranberries

Orange twists

Dissolve gelatin and sugar in boiling water. Drain pineapple, reserving juice; set pineapple aside. Add water to pineapple juice to measure one cup; stir in lemon juice.

Stir juice mixture into gelatin mixture; chill until consistency of unbeaten egg white. Add ground cranberries and oranges, celery and walnuts to gelatin mixture and blend well. Pour gelatin into a lightly oiled 10-cup mold and chill until firm.

Unmold salad onto a serving platter lined with lettuce leaves. Garnish with Sugar-Frosted Cranberries and orange twists.

Sugar-Frosted Cranberries

2 tablespoons water

1 tablespoon pasteurized egg white or liquid egg substitute

1 cup sugar

1 (12-ounce) bag fresh cranberries

In a medium bowl, stir together water and egg product until blended but not whipped. Spread sugar on a rimmed baking sheet. Coat cranberries in egg mixture, then roll them in sugar until well-coated. Dry at room temperature for two hours.

Yield: 15 to 18 servings

TIP: If your gelatin mold does not have a size stamped on it, you can determine its capacity by simply measuring the number of cups of water it will hold.

BRINING

Brining is the key to preparing and serving a very juicy turkey. Taste a brined turkey side-by-side with a non-brined bird and you, too, will be a convert.

An amazing bit of culinary chemistry takes place when you soak a turkey or chicken for a few hours in a solution of salt and sugar. This combination causes the meat to actually absorb additional water, resulting in a more juicy bird at the holiday table.

The salt also adds a nice savory flavor deep into the meat that you cannot get by simply seasoning the surface. Brining also seems to make the bird cook more uniformly, which means there should be fewer problems with pink meat near the bone and dry meat on the outside.

It's this easy:

2   **quarts cold water**

1   **cup kosher salt**

1   **cup brown sugar**

Combine brining ingredients and pour over meat. Allow it to soak for 12 to 24 hours.

TIP: You may use a clean cooler to do your brining, especially if the turkey is a large one. If that is the case, you will want to double the amount of the brining ingredients. Also, creatively add any of your favorite spices that you think will enhance the flavor of the finished dish.

BRINED TURKEY ROASTED WITH ROSEMARY AND THYME

1   **(13-pound) fresh or frozen turkey, thawed and brined**

Kosher salt and freshly ground pepper

Sprigs of fresh thyme or 2 teaspoons dried thyme

3   **sprigs fresh rosemary**

2   **sticks unsalted butter**

Sage Butter (page 26)

Preheat oven to 325 degrees. Place turkey in a large roasting pan, breast side up. Reserve any packaged giblets for later use. Sprinkle turkey generously with salt and pepper.

Insert sprigs of thyme and rosemary into the cavity and under the breast skin. Place one stick of butter in the neck cavity and one in the lower cavity. Tent the breast with folded foil and roast the turkey for 20 minutes per pound or until done, removing foil tent about 30 minutes before roasting is complete.

Let turkey stand at room temperature for 20 minutes before carving. Reserve pan drippings for later use in making gravy.

To add further flavor to the roasted bird, rub the outside with Sage Butter before cooking.

Do not use a pre-basted turkey for this preparation, and purchase a fresh one whenever possible.

SISTER *Says!*

The number of hours to cook and internal temperature instructions are usually printed on the packaging for the turkey. Follow these, as well as the safe-handling suggestions, for a bird that is cooked to perfection and safe for everyone.

OLD-FASHIONED CORNBREAD DRESSING

Those of us whose culinary tastes were born in the south were probably raised eating Cornbread Dressing alongside the holiday turkey. If we were not fortunate enough to have a revered family cook write an actual recipe for us, then we may have spent many a holiday trying hard to replicate the savory dish of our childhood. Whether your family uses a lot of sage, or none at all; whether the top is smooth or has crispy bits of browned cornbread rising off the surface is all moot.

Because however your family made it and whatever their "secret" was is what made it divine and memorable to you. If you don't have your own recipe, we share our versions with the hope you will love it or be able to adapt it to the taste that draws you back to your grandmother's table, where the dressing was always the "best in the world"!

10	cups crumbled cornbread
1	pan Sister Schubert's® Parker House Style Rolls, torn into small pieces

Turkey broth for dressing and gravy (see page 26)

6	eggs, lightly beaten
½	cup unsalted butter
2	onions, peeled and chopped
2	cups chopped celery
2	tablespoons minced fresh parsley

Salt and pepper to taste

3	tablespoons chopped fresh sage
3	tablespoons chopped fresh thyme

Add cornbread and rolls or white bread to a large mixing bowl. Add reserved broth, a little at a time, and stir mixture to desired consistency; you will learn to use your own judgment on this. However, it should be wet enough to see "swirls" in the mixture behind the spoon as it is being stirred. Add beaten eggs and mix well.

Meanwhile, preheat oven to 350 degrees. Grease a 3-quart baking dish and set aside.

Melt butter in a large skillet over medium heat and sauté chopped onions and celery until tender and translucent. Allow vegetables to cool slightly and stir into cornbread mixture along with parsley. Add salt, pepper, sage and thyme.

Spoon mixture into prepared dish and bake for one hour.

Yield: 10 to 12 servings

 I always add 2 cups finely chopped bell pepper, sautéed with onion and celery, to my dressing.

 For my traditional savory dressing, instead of Sister's rolls (which are saved for the table) I use 8 cups of torn white bread.

OLD-FASHIONED
CORNBREAD DRESSING
GREAT GRAVY

GREAT GRAVY

½ cup unsalted butter

8 tablespoons olive oil

1 cup all-purpose flour

2 tablespoons Worcestershire

Pan drippings, reserved from roasting turkey (see page 23)

4 cups turkey or chicken broth

Salt and pepper to taste

Over medium heat, heat butter and olive oil in a heavy pot or deep skillet. Add flour and whisk until completely blended, about three or four minutes; flour should be slightly browned. Stir in Worcestershire and reserved pan drippings; add broth a little at a time, whisking constantly to prevent lumps. Continue cooking gravy until it reaches the desired consistency. Salt and pepper to taste.

Turkey Stock

Turkey giblets, reserved from earlier preparation

2 large onions, peeled and quartered

3 ribs celery, including tops, cut into large dice

Salt and pepper to taste

Pour 4 quarts cold water into a large saucepan. Add turkey giblets (except liver) and any extra skin or parts, along with quartered onion, celery stalks and tops, salt and pepper. Cover and bring to a boil; reduce heat and simmer for about one hour. Strain broth, discard solids, and set aside.

SPICED CRANBERRIES

4 cups fresh cranberries

2 cups water

3 cups sugar

1 teaspoon cinnamon

½ teaspoon ground cloves

Pinch of ground ginger or 1 teaspoon grated fresh ginger

2 teaspoons orange zest, optional

Wash cranberries and drain; set aside.

Combine remaining ingredients in a large saucepan and bring to a boil. Add cranberries; cook about eight minutes or until cranberry skins begin to pop. Reduce heat and simmer one hour, stirring often. Remove from heat and cool.

Chill until ready to serve.

SAGE BUTTER

1 stick unsalted butter, softened

2 tablespoons sage

1 teaspoon salt

1 teaspoon pepper

Add all ingredients to a small mixing bowl and stir thoroughly with a fork to blend.

CITRUS SUNSHINE SWEET POTATOES

8	medium sweet potatoes
1	cup butter, softened
1 ½	cups sugar
1	cup milk
6	eggs, lightly beaten
⅓	cup frozen orange juice concentrate, thawed
	Grated rind of 1 orange
1	teaspoon vanilla
1	teaspoon cinnamon
½	teaspoon nutmeg
½	teaspoon ground cloves
1	cup chopped pecans
2	tablespoons butter, melted

Place potatoes in a large pot and cover completely with cold water. Bring to a boil; reduce heat and simmer until potatoes are tender when pierced with a fork, about 40 minutes. Drain and cool.

Preheat oven to 350 degrees. Butter a large casserole dish and set aside.

Slip skins off slightly cooled potatoes and add them to a large mixing bowl. Add all remaining ingredients except pecans and melted butter and whip with electric mixer until well blended. Spoon potato mixture into prepared casserole dish.

Toss pecans with melted butter and sprinkle over potatoes. Bake for one hour.

Yield: 10 to 12 servings

SISTER Says! This dish may be prepared the day before serving. Cover with plastic wrap and refrigerate overnight. Take out of refrigerator an hour before baking; bake just before serving.

Laughter is brightest where food is best.

IRISH PROVERB

SISTER'S ORIGINAL PARKER HOUSE ROLLS

1   package active dry yeast

1½   cups warm water (105 to 115 degrees)

5   cups sifted all-purpose flour, divided

½   cup sugar

1½   teaspoons salt

½   cup shortening, melted and cooled to 105 to 115 degrees

2   large eggs, lightly beaten

½   cup butter, melted

1¼   cups all-purpose flour

Combine yeast and warm water in a 2-cup liquid measuring cup; let stand five minutes.

Combine 4 cups sifted flour, sugar and salt in a large bowl. Stir in yeast mixture and shortening. Add eggs and remaining 1 cup sifted flour; stir vigorously until well blended. Dough will be soft and sticky. Brush or lightly rub dough with some of the melted butter. Cover loosely with a damp tea towel and let rise in a warm place (85 degrees), free from drafts, for about 1½ hours or until doubled in bulk.

Grease four 8-inch round foil cake pans and set aside.

Sift ¾ cup flour in a thick layer evenly over work surface; turn dough out onto flour. Dough will still be soft. Sift remaining ½ cup flour evenly over dough. Roll dough to ½-inch thickness; brush off excess flour.

Cut dough using a 2-inch floured biscuit cutter. Pull each round into an oval, approximately 2½ inches long. Dip one side of the oval into melted butter. Fold oval in half with buttered side facing outward. The floured side will form the famous "Parker House pocket."

For each pan, place the folds of 10 rolls against the side of the prepared pan, pressing center fronts of rolls together to seal. Place five rolls in inner circle and one roll in the center for a total of 16 rolls in each pan.

Cover pans loosely with a damp tea towel and let rise in a warm, draft-free space for one hour or until doubled in bulk.

To bake, preheat oven to 400 degrees. Bake rolls, uncovered, for 12 to 15 minutes or until tops are lightly browned.

Yield: 64 rolls

TO FREEZE: Bake as directed. Cool rolls on baking sheet, cover with foil and place in freezer. Once rolls are frozen, place in zip-lock freezer bags and return to freezer. Keeps well for up to three months, but don't expect to have enough left to freeze!

SISTER Says! If you are short on time, Sister Shubert's® Parker House Style Rolls, found in the freezer section of your grocery store, are a convenient and delicious option.

CONFETTI ROASTED VEGETABLES

2	crookneck squash, sliced
2	zucchini, sliced
2	red peppers, cut into strips
2	green peppers, cut into strips
2	yellow peppers, cut into strips
2	red onions, sliced
6	cloves garlic, minced
½	cup olive oil
1	tablespoon minced rosemary
1	tablespoon minced thyme

Preheat oven to 400 degrees. Combine all vegetables in a large bowl. Add garlic and olive oil and toss well to coat. Stir in rosemary and thyme and toss again. Pour vegetables on rimmed baking pans and roast 20 to 25 minutes.

Yield: 8 to 10 servings

 SISTER Says! These may be prepared ahead of serving time and reheated or served at room temperature.

Eat, drink and be merry.

ISAIAH 22:13

QUICK AND EASY CARAMEL PIE

2	cups brown sugar, packed	4	eggs, lightly beaten
1	cup chopped pecans	2	tablespoons unsalted butter, melted
2	tablespoons all-purpose flour		
2	teaspoons vanilla extract	1	unbaked pie shell
2	cups heavy cream		Meringue for topping, if desired (see page 33)

Preheat oven to 350 degrees. Mix filling ingredients well and pour into pie shell. Bake for 45 minutes or until set. Cool slightly if planning to cover with meringue.

PUMPKIN MOUSSE

Crust

1 ½ cups graham cracker crumbs (about 14 crackers)

½ cup light brown sugar

1 stick unsalted butter, melted

Stir together cracker crumbs and sugar with a fork; pour in butter and continue to blend. Press mixture into a tart pan and use the bottom of a measuring cup to firmly tamp it down. Set aside while preparing filling.

Filling

1 package unflavored gelatin

¼ cup water

½ cup half-and-half

1 (18-ounce) can pumpkin purée

1 cup light brown sugar

¾ teaspoon salt

½ teaspoon cinnamon

¼ teaspoon nutmeg

¾ cup egg yolks

1 ripe banana, mashed

Zest of 1 orange, divided

Soften gelatin in water and set aside.

In a large heavy saucepan, gently heat half-and-half, pumpkin, sugar, salt and spices. Stir well to blend and add egg yolks slowly to the mixture, whisking constantly.

Remove from heat and stir in reserved gelatin. Fold in banana and half of orange zest, blending well. Cool slightly and pour pumpkin mixture into prepared crust.

Topping

1 cup heavy cream

3 tablespoons sugar

1 teaspoon vanilla extract

Reserved orange zest

In a small chilled bowl, beat cream until soft peaks form. Gradually beat in sugar and vanilla until the cream reaches a slightly stiffer stage.

Spoon topping around the outside edge of the Mousse, reserving some for the center. Sprinkle top with remaining orange zest and chill before serving.

FABULOUS CARAMEL PIE

PECAN PIE

FABULOUS CARAMEL PIE

8   tablespoons cornstarch

2 ½ cups whole milk, divided

1 ½ cups granulated sugar, divided

    Pinch of salt

6   egg yolks, lightly beaten

1   teaspoon vanilla extract

⅓   cup unsalted butter, melted

1   pre-baked pie shell

Meringue

In a heavy-bottomed saucepan, add cornstarch and ½ cup milk and stir until smooth.

Add remaining milk, ½ cup sugar and salt. Cook over medium heat, stirring constantly until mixture thickens. Stir a small amount of the hot mixture into the beaten eggs to temper them. Continue adding small amounts of hot mixture until egg mixture is just warm.

Add egg mixture into the hot milk mixture and cook for an additional three minutes.

Place remaining cup of sugar in a heavy saucepan or copper sauté pan. Heat over medium-high heat, whisking until sugar melts and turns a rich caramel color. Add to milk custard mixture in a slow, steady stream, whisking until very thick.

Stir in vanilla and butter. Pour mixture into baked pie shell.

Let cool for 20 minutes while making Meringue.

. . . .

Meringue

6   egg whites

½   teaspoon cream of tartar

6   tablespoons sugar

1   teaspoon vanilla extract

Preheat oven to 350 degrees.

Whip egg whites until frothy. Add cream of tartar and whip until egg whites stand in stiff peaks, but are not dry. Beat in sugar very slowly. Beat in vanilla.

Cover pie with some of the meringue. Take care to spread the meringue so that it touches the crust all the way around. After you have covered the caramel filling well, pile on the rest of the meringue and make decorative swirls with the back of a spoon. Bake until the meringue begins to brown lightly, about 15 minutes.

Let cool completely. Refrigerate at least one hour before slicing.

AVOIDING THE DREADED SHRINKING MERINGUE

When a meringue is baked in the oven, the tightening of the egg-white proteins causes the meringue to shrink. It also makes the meringue difficult to cut smoothly. My solution to this problem is to add a little cornstarch paste to the meringue. Cornstarch prevents the egg-white bonds from tightening (in the same way that it prevents eggs from curdling in a pastry cream) so the meringue doesn't shrink. This tender meringue with starch cuts like a dream.

FLAKY PIE CRUST

2 ½ cups all-purpose flour

½ teaspoon salt

¾ cup cold unsalted butter, cut into small cubes

½ cup cold vegetable shortening, cut into small cubes

In the bowl of a food processor, combine flour and salt. Add cold butter and process mixture until it resembles coarse meal. Add shortening and process mixture until it resembles meal. Add very cold water, a tablespoon at a time, until mixture forms a soft, but not sticky, dough.

Remove mixture from the processor bowl and form dough into a ball. If making a double-crust pie, or one with a lattice top crust, divide the dough into two balls, one slightly larger than the other. If making two single-crust pies, halve the dough.

The dough may be rolled out immediately or kept, wrapped in wax paper and chilled, for up to two days.

Yield: One double 9-inch crust or two single 9-inch crusts.

TIP: This easy and delicious recipe can be used for any of your favorite pie fillings.

PECAN PIE

1 cup broken pecan pieces

1 (9-inch) Flaky Pie Crust, unbaked

½ cup unsalted butter, melted

3 eggs, lightly beaten

1 cup granulated sugar

1 cup brown sugar, packed

1 cup dark corn syrup or cane syrup if available

2 teaspoons vanilla extract

Pinch of salt

Preheat oven to 325 degrees. Sprinkle pecans in bottom of pie shell and set aside.

Mix together melted butter, eggs, sugar, brown sugar, corn syrup, vanilla and salt; blend well. Pour mixture into pie shell, over pecans. Bake for one hour or until filling is set.

Yield: 8 servings

SISTER Says! After 30 minutes of baking, cover outer edge of crust with strips of foil to prevent over browning. Or as Betty says, "You can get one of those gizmos from the cooking store to cover the outside crust!"

CREAMY TURKEY SOUP AND
AVOCADO GRAPEFRUIT SALAD
WITH LEMON VINAIGRETTE

MENU

Cranberry-Goat Cheese Spread

Creamy Turkey Soup

Avocado Grapefruit Salad with
Lemon Vinaigrette

Hazelnut Mousse

Holiday Celebrations

DAY AFTER THANKSGIVING

Lunch

This kind of fare just doesn't deserve to be called "leftovers"! Much of the joy of the Thanksgiving feast lies in the fact that plenty of food will be available the following day.

Whether you plan to get an early start on Christmas shopping or stay snug at home watching football on TV, the refrigerator is well-stocked when you're ready for an afternoon repast. But some of us have had enough of turkey sandwiches and want something different to serve before the weekend arrives. This menu is for you! Leave the crowded malls for the comfort of your home, with a delightful lunch to help you wind down in style.

CRANBERRY-GOAT CHEESE SPREAD

6   ounces goat cheese, softened

4   tablespoons unsalted butter,
    softened

3   tablespoons whole-berry
    cranberry sauce

In a medium bowl, combine goat cheese and butter. Beat at medium speed with an electric mixer until smooth. Add cranberry sauce to mixture, beating until well combined. Cover tightly and refrigerate until ready to serve. Serve with assorted crackers.

Yield: 8 servings

AVOCADO GRAPEFRUIT SALAD WITH LEMON VINAIGRETTE

Lemon Vinaigrette

¼   cup lemon juice

1   tablespoon sugar

1   tablespoon Dijon mustard

½   cup olive oil

½   teaspoon salt

½   teaspoon pepper

Whisk together all ingredients until well-blended.

Salad

8   pieces Boston lettuce

4   avocados

4   grapefruit

Place one lettuce leaf on each of eight salad plates.

Slice avocados lengthwise. Carefully twist and pull sides apart. Remove pit and scoop avocado from shell with a tablespoon. Dip avocados in Lemon Vinaigrette to prevent darkening.

Section grapefruit and divide evenly on lettuce-lined plates. Slice avocados and place over grapefruit pieces. Drizzle plates with vinaigrette to serve.

 SISTER *Says!* Most grocery stores offer a variety of jarred grapefruit sections that will taste fine and save some time in preparing this dish. Just be sure to drain them well before constructing the salad.

CREAMY TURKEY SOUP

1	turkey carcass, cut into pieces
2	ribs celery, chopped
1	large onion, chopped
2	carrots, chopped
¼	teaspoon crumbled dried tarragon
2	bay leaves
1	tablespoon soy sauce
15	peppercorns
1	teaspoon salt
12	cups water
1	cup heavy cream, divided
½	cup cornstarch
	Salt and pepper to taste
¼	cup port

In a kettle, combine turkey carcass, celery, onion, carrots, tarragon, bay leaves, soy sauce, peppercorns, salt and water. Bring liquid to a boil, skim foam and simmer mixture for three hours, covered.

In a bowl, whisk together ½ cup cream and cornstarch until smooth. Strain soup mixture into a large pot. Over high heat, reduce liquid by half. Reduce heat to moderately low, stir cornstarch mixture again and add it to soup in a steady stream while whisking. Simmer for one minute or until it is slightly thickened. Season to taste with salt and pepper.

Spoon ½ tablespoon port into each of eight warmed soup bowls and ladle soup into bowls.

Yield: 8 servings (about 9 cups of soup)

NOTE: Ideally, the carcass should be from a small turkey, about 12 pounds. If your turkey was larger, you may not want to use quite all of it.

HAZELNUT MOUSSE

1 ½	cups heavy cream, divided
¾	cup Nutella chocolate-hazelnut spread
	Fresh strawberries for garnish
	Confectioner's' sugar for garnish

In a medium bowl, combine ¾ cup cream and chocolate-hazelnut spread. Beat at medium-high speed with an electric mixer until creamy. Add remaining cream, beating until stiff peaks form. Spoon into serving dishes and garnish with strawberries and sift confectioners' sugar over the top, if desired.

Holiday Celebrations

FESTIVE
Christmas
DINNER

Christmas is a celebration of the birth of Jesus, but also it is a time for family and friends to gather together for food and fellowship. For Betty and Bill, the days leading up to Christmas provide opportunities for hosting everything from open houses, brunches, and cookie exchanges to an early Christmas gift exchange. Crystal angels adorn the tables, wound about with gold ribbons amid greenery and silver candlesticks. Candlelight flickers from every room and the family gathers from far and wide. When Christmas Eve finally arrives, a magical warmth spreads from the fireplace to the busy kitchen and drifts gently over their home.

As Christmas Eve church services conclude, the tables are laid and the children giggle in anticipation of what the night holds for them. Whether formal or casual, the celebration always promises to be joyous!

MENU

Mushroom Pâté

Gourmet Goat Cheese Spread

Slow-Roasted Prime Rib

Spinach Salad with Mango-
Ginger Chutney Dressing

Three-Cheese Potato Gratin

Sister Schubert's®
Parker House Style Rolls

Charlotte aux Fraises

Flaming Cherries Jubilee

WINE SUGGESTIONS:
Cabernet Sauvignon
from Napa Valley

PRIME RIB PRIMER

Rich and flavorful (as well as pricey), prime rib is typically reserved for special-occasion meals.

ABOUT THE CUT: A prime rib roast, or standing rib roast, is cut from the back of the upper rib section of the steer. It is usually comprised of seven ribs.

ABOUT THE GRADE: Prime is the best USDA grade of beef available, having the most marbling (flecks of fat interspersed in the meat) and, therefore, the best flavor and tenderness.

SLOW-ROASTED PRIME RIB

1   (3-bone) beef rib roast, about 8 pounds

3   tablespoons sea salt

1½ tablespoons coarsely cracked black pepper

1   tablespoon extra-virgin olive oil

8   sprigs fresh rosemary

8   sprigs fresh thyme

10 cloves garlic, smashed and peeled

3   tablespoons unsalted butter, cut into ½-inch cubes

Take the beef out of the refrigerator 2 hours before cooking so it can come to room temperature. Season the meat on all sides with the sea salt and cracked black pepper.

Position rack in the center of the oven and preheat oven to 450 degrees.

Heat a 12-inch skillet over high heat for 1 minute. Swirl in the olive oil and, when the oil puts off its first wisp of smoke, place the beef in the pan, and sear it on all the outer sides until well browned, 6 to 8 minutes total. Use tongs to flip the beef; be careful of splattering oil. Transfer roast, bone side down, to a large roasting pan with rack. Add ¾ cup water to the bottom of the pan to help prevent drippings from smoking. Arrange the rosemary, thyme, garlic, and butter evenly on top.

TURN OVEN OFF BUT DO NOT OPEN THE DOOR TO THE OVEN. Leave roast undisturbed in oven for 2 hours for rare and 2½ hours for medium rare.

Remove from oven and baste with pan drippings. Let stand for 10 to 15 minutes before carving.

Yield: 6 to 8 servings

Meat Temperatures & Approximate Roasting Time

120-135 degrees for rare – 1¼ hours

140-145 degrees for medium – 1½ hours

155-160 degrees for well done – 2 hours

NOTE: If you have the luxury of using the services of a butcher, request that the roast be cut from the small or loin end and that it is prime.

SPINACH SALAD WITH MANGO-GINGER CHUTNEY DRESSING

Dressing

½ cup vegetable oil

¼ cup mango-ginger chutney

1 teaspoon curry powder

1 teaspoon dry mustard

½ teaspoon salt

2 tablespoons fresh lemon juice

1 teaspoon sugar

Combine all dressing ingredients in a screw-top jar; shake vigorously to mix well. Can be made ahead and refrigerated. Bring to room temperature before tossing with other ingredients.

Salad

2 bunches (about 1 ½ pounds) small leaf spinach, stemmed, washed and patted dry

2 apples, cored, halved crosswise and thinly sliced

1 cup toasted pecans

½ to ¾ cup raisins

½ cup chopped green onion

Combine spinach, apples, pecans, raisins and onion in a large salad bowl. Toss salad with dressing immediately before serving.

Yield: 4 to 6 servings

TIP: Toasting nuts enhances their flavor, especially when using them for salads or any uncooked purpose. Preheat oven to 350 degrees. Spread nuts in a single layer on baking sheet. Place in oven, stirring every 3 to 5 minutes. Toast for 8-12 minutes; the color will be slightly darker and the nuts will begin to smell fragrant. Because of their high fat content, they will burn easily, so be sure to watch them carefully when toasting.

GOURMET GOAT CHEESE SPREAD

4 ounces goat cheese (Montrachet or good chèvre), at room temperature

1 (8-ounce) package cream cheese, softened

⅔ cup coarsely chopped walnuts or pine nuts

4 oil-packed, sun-dried tomato halves, drained, coarsely chopped

1 large clove garlic, coarsely chopped

1 teaspoon extra-virgin olive oil

¼ teaspoon minced fresh thyme

Salt and coarsely ground black pepper to taste

Combine all ingredients in the bowl of a food processor. Pulse until blended but still slightly chunky. Spoon mixture into a serving bowl or place in a small bowl lined with plastic wrap. Chill for at least ten minutes or until firm.

If lining bowl with plastic wrap, unmold onto a serving plate; otherwise, serve from bowl with your favorite crackers or crostini.

Note: Cheese spread can be made ahead and will hold in refrigerator for 3 days.

Yield: 2 cups

Great cooking is the source of great happiness.

ESCOFFIER

MUSHROOM PATE

2 tablespoons unsalted butter

1 pound fresh mushrooms

2 (8-ounce) packages cream cheese, softened

1 teaspoon garlic salt

Melt butter in a medium skillet. Add mushrooms and sauté until liquids dissipate. Place all ingredients in the bowl of a food processor and pulse until mixture is smooth. Spoon mixture into a small serving bowl; cover and refrigerate.

When ready to serve, garnish as desired and serve with small wheat crackers.

Yield: 2 cups

THREE-CHEESE POTATO GRATIN

2 pounds Yukon gold or russet potatoes

1 ½ cups heavy cream

1 ½ cups whole milk

1 teaspoon coarse salt

⅛ teaspoon freshly ground black pepper

Generous pinch of freshly grated nutmeg

2 cloves garlic, peeled and lightly flattened

½ cup freshly grated Parmigiano-Reggiano cheese

1 cup freshly grated Gruyère or Swiss cheese

2 ounces fresh goat cheese, crumbled

Preheat oven to 400 degrees. Lightly butter a 2 ½- to 3-quart casserole dish and set aside.

Peel potatoes and cut into ⅛-inch slices. Add potatoes to a large heavy-bottomed saucepan; stir in cream, milk, salt, pepper, nutmeg and garlic. Cook mixture over medium-high heat until boiling, stirring occasionally. Remove garlic cloves and discard. Pour mixture into prepared baking dish and top with cheeses.

Bake until top is deep golden brown and potatoes are very tender when pierced with a knife, about 40 minutes. Before serving, allow potatoes to cool until they are very warm, but not hot, about 15 minutes.

Yield: 10-15 servings

CHARLOTTE AUX FRAISES

2 envelopes unflavored gelatin

¾ cup water at room temperature

½ cup kirsch

½ cup water

¾ cup light brown sugar, firmly packed

1 pan Sister Schubert's® Parker House Style Rolls, split

2 cups whole milk

1½ cups granulated sugar

2 pints heavy cream

6 large egg whites

¼ cup sweet sherry

1 pint fresh strawberries, blackberries or raspberries

Fresh mint leaves for garnish

Dissolve unflavored gelatin in ¾ cup warm water and set aside.

In a small, deep bowl, combine kirsch, ½ cup water and brown sugar; stir to blend completely. Dip each roll half in kirsch mixture to saturate and arrange in the bottom and up the sides of a trifle or similar crystal bowl. Set aside to prepare filling.

Combine milk and granulated sugar in a saucepan and, over medium heat, stir until sugar dissolves completely. Add reserved gelatin mixture and stir until it is dissolved into milk mixture. Remove from heat and chill mixture in refrigerator until it begins to thicken, about 20 minutes.

Meanwhile, whip heavy cream until just before reaching stiff peaks. In a separate bowl, beat egg whites to the same consistency, just before reaching stiff peaks.

Remove gelatin mixture from refrigerator and gently fold in whipped cream, beaten egg whites and sherry. Spoon mixture over rolls in trifle bowl and chill overnight.

To serve, top with fresh berries of choice and garnish with mint leaves.

NOTE: If fresh fruit is not available, a large jar of maraschino cherries, drained, may be used to garnish the dish.

SISTER Says! Nall and I have very happy memories of this fabulous dessert. His mother used sweet biscuits and my mother always used ladyfingers. Now I use my sweet rolls.

FLAMING CHERRIES JUBILEE

1 can pitted black sweet cherries

1 tablespoon sugar

1 tablespoon cornstarch

1 teaspoon cinnamon

¼ cup kirsch or brandy, warmed

Vanilla bean ice cream

Drain cherries, reserving the liquid. In small saucepan or copper skillet, mix sugar, cornstarch and cinnamon. Gradually stir in all reserved liquid. Cook on medium about 3 minutes, stirring constantly, until thickened. Add cherries and continue cooking until heated throughout. Pour warm brandy over top of cherry mixture. Using a long match or butane lighter, carefully ignite brandy. Working quickly, using a long-handle spoon, carefully scoop flaming cherries over ice cream. Serve immediately.

Yield: 6 servings

BETTY'S Best! For easier, and quicker, serving, spoon ice cream into individual dishes ahead of time. Set them on a tray and put them in the freezer. They will be ready to serve immediately once the cherry mixture is ready. The recipe is easily doubled for a larger party and makes quite a dramatic presentation!

SANTA WATCH
Soup Supper

Christmas in Vence is a peaceful time to reflect on the passing year, remember the message of Christ's life, and gather with friends to celebrate with a festive dinner. Nall prefers to make his wreaths and home décor from natural materials—his country home welcomes one and all with fresh greenery and glistening indoor trees. When friends bring their children, everyone plays games and enjoys dessert before receiving handmade gifts; nothing from the store will do! There might be a bonfire and roasted chestnuts to share before the children go home to await Père Noël. When he is home in Alabama for the holidays, the family gathers, and he and his cousins reminisce about their lives since childhood. On Christmas Eve, Nall toasts the memory of his parents, Mary and Joe, and his wonderful grandmother, Miss Lucy, gone but never forgotten. Wherever he is, the best part of the day is a call to his many friends across the globe for a brief "Joyeux Noël" to one and all.

WASSAIL

1   (32-ounce can) cranberry juice cocktail

1   cup water

⅓   cup frozen orange-pineapple juice concentrate, thawed

2   sticks cinnamon

2   whole cloves

    Orange peel curls

In a large saucepan, stir together cranberry juice cocktail, water, juice concentrate, cinnamon sticks and cloves. Bring to a boil; reduce heat and cover. Simmer for 10 minutes. Cool slightly and strain into a small punch bowl.

If desired, add a cinnamon stick to each cup before serving.

Yield: 10 servings

MENU

Nuts and Bolts

Wassail

Stand-Up Caesar Salad

Turkey Rolls

Sister's Slow Cooker White Chili

Nall's Seahorse Chowder

Chicken and Sausage Gumbo

Sour Cream Cornbread

Chocolate Italian Cream Cake

NUTS AND BOLTS

2   sticks unsalted butter

2 ½   tablespoons Worcestershire sauce

1 ¼   teaspoons garlic powder

1 ⅛   teaspoons Tabasco sauce

1   teaspoon paprika

1   small box round oat cereal

1   box rice squares cereal

1   box corn squares cereal

1   box wheat squares cereal

1   bag pretzel sticks

4   cups toasted pecans, lightly salted

Preheat oven to 300 degrees. Line 2 large jelly-roll pans with parchment or foil and set aside.

In a small saucepan over medium heat, melt butter. Add Worcestershire, garlic powder, Tabasco sauce and paprika. Stir well to blend.

Add all cereals and pretzels to a large mixing bowl and toss well. Pour butter mixture over cereal and toss again to blend thoroughly. Spread half of mixture on each of the jelly-roll pans; cover loosely with foil. Bake for 1 ½ hours, stirring mixture every 20 minutes. About a half hour before cooking is complete, stir in pecans and any additional nuts preferred.

To make a good soup, the pot must only simmer or smile.

FRENCH PROVERB

STAND-UP CAESAR SALAD

2	heads romaine lettuce or romaine hearts	Wash and dry lettuce. Place leaves on a baking sheet lined with a tea towel. Place sheet in refrigerator and allow lettuce to crisp before serving.

Dressing

1	teaspoon grated lemon rind	Combine the lemon rind, juice, garlic and vinegar in a small bowl and whisk well. Slowly add olive oil, whisking until smooth. Add pepper and salt. Finally, whisk in mayonnaise until mixture is smooth. Cover and refrigerate.
3	tablespoons fresh lemon juice	
2	cloves garlic, minced	
1	tablespoon white wine vinegar	
⅔	cup olive oil	To prepare, toss romaine leaves lightly with dressing. Add leaves to 8-ounce crystal highball glasses, allowing one leaf to show above the rim. Add crostini as added interest.
1	teaspoon freshly ground black pepper	
½	teaspoon salt	Eat with fingers or fork.
¼	cup mayonnaise	

NALL'S SEAHORSE CHOWDER

4	slices bacon
¼	cup olive oil
1	medium onion, chopped (1 cup)
4	stalks celery, washed and finely chopped (2 cups)
1	teaspoon ground nutmeg
1 ½	teaspoons Tony Chachere's Original Creole seasoning, divided
1 ½	teaspoons Old Bay seasoning, divided
1 ½	teaspoons red pepper flakes, divided
8	ears fresh corn, kernels cut from cob, or 4 cups frozen corn

1	large russet potato, scrubbed, peeled and chopped into small cubes
1	cup chicken broth
3	cups half-and-half
1	pound large fresh shrimp, peeled, deveined and cut into thirds
¼	cup unsalted butter, cubed
2	teaspoons all-purpose flour

Salt and pepper

In a large skillet, cook bacon until crisp. Remove bacon; set aside. Add ¼ cup olive oil, onion and celery to bacon drippings. Sauté about 4 minutes or until onion is translucent. Add nutmeg and 1 teaspoon each of Tony's, Old Bay and red pepper flakes. Add corn and potato; continue to cook for 5 minutes, stirring often. Transfer vegetable mixture to a large stockpot. Add broth and half-and-half and stir to mix. On low to medium heat, cook, covered, for 20 minutes or until potato cubes are tender. Watch carefully and stir occasionally to avoid scorching.

While the base is cooking, in large skillet, melt butter and add remaining seasoning and shrimp. Sauté shrimp for 3 to 5 minutes, or until pink and no longer translucent. Remove shrimp to plate and set aside. Reduce heat to low and add flour to drippings, stirring constantly until of a runny paste consistency. Drizzle paste into chowder; mix. Add shrimp to chowder and cook another 5 minutes. Salt and pepper to taste.

Serve in bowls or mugs with crumbled bacon on top.

Yield: 4 to 6 hearty servings

SISTER'S SLOW COOKER WHITE CHILI

1   pound Great Northern beans, soaked per package directions

2   pounds boneless, skinless chicken breasts

1   medium onion, chopped

3   cloves garlic, minced

2   tablespoons chili powder

1 ½ teaspoons cayenne pepper

½   teaspoon salt

1   (16-ounce) can reduced-sodium chicken broth

1   cup water

Drain and rinse soaked beans; put in a medium saucepan and cover with cold water. Bring to a boil, reduce heat and allow to simmer 20 minutes. Drain and discard water. Add beans to the bowl of a slow cooker.

Cut chicken into 1-inch pieces and add to beans. Stir in all remaining ingredients and mix well. Cover and cook on low for 10 hours or on high for 6 hours.

Yield: 8 servings

For extra flavor and color, brown chicken cubes lightly in olive oil before adding to the beans. Also, the chicken breasts may be added whole and cooked with the chili. When ready to serve, remove chicken to a plate and shred meat with 2 forks before returning it to the pot.

BETTY'S MICROWAVE ROUX
(This easy microwave roux can be the base of any recipe calling for one.)

⅔   cup all-purpose flour

⅔   cup vegetable oil or strained bacon grease

Mix flour and oil together in a 4-cup ovenproof glass measuring cup. Microwave on full power for 6 to 7 minutes. Roux will be light brown at this time and will need to cook 30 to 60 seconds longer in order to reach a dark brown. At this point, vegetables (onion, celery, peppers) can be added and the roux cooked on high power for 3 minutes. Add to other ingredients and proceed with recipe. Watch carefully; do not over brown roux.

TURKEY ROLLS

2   pans Sister Schubert's® Parker House Style Rolls

1   (8-ounce) jar orange marmalade

1   pound turkey, thinly sliced

Preheat oven to 350 degrees. Remove rolls from pan, without separating them individually. With a serrated knife, carefully slice rolls in half, horizontally, creating a top and bottom piece. Spread orange marmalade on the inside of the top piece. Top the bottom with turkey slices. Close rolls and return to pans. Cover loosely with foil.

Bake for 15 to 20 minutes or until thoroughly heated. Remove from pan, and separate individually. You may need to slice into individual sandwiches. Serve warm and enjoy.

Yield: 32 rolls

SOUR CREAM CORNBREAD

¼   cup unsalted butter

1   cup cream-style corn

1   cup sour cream

1   cup self-rising cornmeal

½   medium onion, grated

2   eggs, lightly beaten

Preheat oven to 350 degrees. Add butter to an 8×8-inch baking dish or an 8-inch cast-iron skillet and place in the oven to melt.

In a small mixing bowl, combine corn, sour cream, cornmeal, onion and eggs and mix well. Carefully remove heated pan from the oven and swirl to coat the pan with butter. Spoon mixture into the prepared pan and return to oven. Bake for 30 to 40 minutes or until brown.

Yield: 10 servings

 SISTER *Says!* For a spicy cornbread, stir 1 can chopped, drained jalapeños into the mixture before baking.

CHICKEN AND SAUSAGE GUMBO

1½   cups vegetable oil

1½   cups all-purpose flour

4   tablespoons vegetable oil

1½   pounds okra, thinly sliced

1   medium onion, chopped

2   stalks celery, chopped

1   medium green pepper, chopped

2   garlic cloves, minced

3   quarts water

1   (28-ounce) can diced tomatoes

½   teaspoon chili powder

½   teaspoon thyme

½   teaspoon basil

3   bay leaves

2   teaspoons salt

1   teaspoon cayenne pepper

1   teaspoon black pepper

½   cup blended chopped parsley and green onion

1   tablespoon Worcestershire sauce

1   pound andouille sausage, cut into ¼-inch slices

2   pounds stewed chicken, cut into bite-sized pieces

1   cup chicken broth

6   cups cooked white rice

Additional chopped parsley and green onion for garnish

2   tablespoons gumbo filé

Heat 1½ cups vegetable oil in a heavy pot or Dutch oven. Add flour slowly to the hot oil, stirring constantly. When thoroughly mixed, lower heat and continue stirring until roux is chocolate brown. Remove from pot to a bowl to stop the cooking. Set aside.

Heat four tablespoons vegetable oil in the same pot. Sauté okra until tender, stirring constantly, about ten minutes. Add onion, celery, green pepper and garlic. Add just enough water to cover. Cook on medium another ten minutes. Add two cups of reserved roux. When dissolving roux to return to pot, dissolve with a bit of warm water so that it will not curdle. Add three quarts water, tomatoes, spices, salt, peppers, parsley, green onions, Worcestershire and sausage. Bring to a low boil, making sure roux is completely dissolved. Lower heat, stir frequently, and simmer for two hours or until vegetables are tender and falling apart. Gently stir in chicken and broth.

To serve, mound hot cooked rice in a serving bowl and spoon gumbo over it. Garnish with chopped parsley and green onion tops. For added zest, sprinkle with gumbo filé. Serve with Sour Cream Cornbread.

CHOCOLATE ITALIAN CREAM CAKE

½ cup unsalted butter, softened

¼ cup canola oil

2 cups sugar

2 large eggs, separated

2 cups all-purpose flour

¼ cup cocoa

1 teaspoon baking soda

1 cup buttermilk

1 tablespoon vanilla extract

1 teaspoon coconut extract

¾ cup flaked coconut

½ cup chopped pecans

4 large egg whites

Chocolate Cream Cheese Icing

Preheat oven to 350 degrees. Coat three 9-inch round cake pans with nonstick cooking spray with flour.

Using an electric mixer, cream butter and oil until smooth. Gradually add sugar and beat until light and fluffy. Add egg yolks, one at a time, beating well after each addition.

Mix flour, cocoa and baking soda together. Add flour mixture to sugar mixture, alternating with buttermilk and ending with flour. Beat after each addition. Add vanilla and coconut extracts, coconut and pecans.

In a separate mixing bowl, beat the 6 egg whites until stiff peaks form. Carefully fold the beaten egg whites into the batter mixture. Pour batter evenly into prepared cake pans.

Bake 20 to 25 minutes or until the top springs back when gently touched. Cool cakes in the pans for 10 minutes, then turn them out on racks to cool thoroughly. Level layers with a knife before frosting. Fill between the layers and frost the top and sides with Chocolate Cream Cheese Icing.

Yield: approximately 16 to 20 slices

 To make cake ahead, place iced cake in a bakery box and wrap with plastic wrap or use a plastic cake carrier. Freeze for up to two months.

Chocolate Cream Cheese Icing

2 (8-ounce) packages cream cheese, softened

6 tablespoons unsalted butter, softened

2 (16-ounce) boxes confectioners' sugar, divided

½ cup cocoa

½ teaspoon ground cinnamon

3 tablespoons heavy cream

2 teaspoons vanilla extract

2 cups chopped pecans

In bowl of electric mixer, beat cream cheese and butter until smooth. Mix together one-half cup confectioners' sugar, cocoa and cinnamon. Add to cream cheese mixture and beat well to blend. Gradually add remaining confectioners' sugar, beating until light. Blend in cream and vanilla. Smooth frosting over layers and then top and sides. Gently press chopped pecans onto the sides of the cake.

NOTE: Before you frost your cake, you will want to make sure it is level. Wait until the cake has cooled, at least one hour. Place cake on a cake board, then place the board on a cake stand. While slowly rotating the cake stand, move the knife back and forth across the top of cake in a sawing motion to remove the crown. Try to keep the knife level as you cut.

 I use vanilla in practically everything, not just baking. Vanilla comes from an orchid plant. There are over 20,000 varieties of orchids and only one, a celadon-colored orchid, produces anything that is edible. Fortunately for us, that is the vanilla bean. Most quality vanilla comes from Madagascar, Africa, and Tahiti. I find most Mexican vanilla to be inferior and do not recommend.

A HEARTWARMING

Brunch

We love entertaining, but the days of planning, preparation, and presentation can be a time challenge before holidays. That is why we love brunch. The menu is delicious, but informal and easy to prepare ahead, leaving us precious time with family and friends, especially at the holidays, when all you need to decorate the table is a big bowl of bright red apples and pomegranates set into a fresh boxwood wreath. Add a few swirls of ribbon and spend some quality time with your guests instead of being tied to the kitchen.

BRUNYON AND LAVENDER BY NALL

CLASSIC SOUTHERN MIMOSA

2 ounces orange juice or blood orange juice

1 teaspoon orange-flavored liqueur (optional)

Champagne

Fresh mint leaves

Pour orange juice of choice into champagne flute; add orange liqueur, if using, and stir well. Carefully pour Champagne down the side of the flute to fill three-quarters full.

Garnish with mint leaves.

Yield: 1 mimosa

MENU

Classic Southern Mimosas

Everyday Granola Parfait

Apple-Pear Coffee Cake

Italian Breakfast Cobbler

Tomato-Herb Mini Frittatas

Praline Bacon

Hot Curried Fruit Compote

George's Chocolate Bread Pudding with Spiced Cream

EVERYDAY GRANOLA PARFAIT

Everyday Granola

3	cups old-fashioned oats
1	cup coarsely chopped pecans
½	cup unsweetened shredded coconut
3	tablespoons brown sugar
¾	teaspoon ground cinnamon
½	teaspoon ground ginger
¼	teaspoon (heaping) salt
⅓	cup honey
2	tablespoons vegetable oil
1	cup assorted dried fruit

Preheat oven to 300 degrees. Line a rimmed baking sheet with parchment and set aside.

Combine oats, pecans, coconut, brown sugar, cinnamon, ginger and salt in a large bowl and mix well. Heat honey and oil in a small saucepan over medium-low heat until smooth, stirring constantly. Add to oat mixture and toss to coat.

Spread mixture on prepared baking sheet and bake for 40 minutes or until golden brown, stirring every 10 minutes. Remove sheet to a wire rack. Stir and let stand until cool; stir in dried fruit.

Store in an airtight container for up to three weeks.

Yield: 5 cups

Parfait

4	cups Everyday Granola
8	cups vanilla yogurt
4	cups sliced strawberries
1 ½	cups blueberries

Spoon ¼ cup granola into the bottom of eight parfait or martini glasses. Add ½ cup yogurt and ¼ cup strawberries. Sprinkle with some of the blueberries. Repeat layers, ending with blueberries.

Yield: 8 servings

Hospitality, warmth, and love are all sitting around the table with us when we share a good meal.

CICERO

APPLE-PEAR COFFEE CAKE

½ cup unsalted butter, softened

1 cup sugar

2 eggs

2 teaspoons vanilla extract

2 cups all-purpose flour

3 teaspoons baking powder

1 teaspoon baking soda

½ teaspoon salt

1 cup sour cream

1 ¼ cups peeled and chopped apple

½ cup peeled and chopped pear

Topping

1 ¼ cups packed brown sugar

1 teaspoon ground cinnamon

3 tablespoons cold unsalted butter, sliced

⅓ cup chopped pecans

Preheat oven to 350 degrees. Grease a 13×9-inch baking dish and set aside.

In a large bowl, cream butter and sugar until light and fluffy. Beat in eggs and vanilla. Combine flour, baking powder, baking soda and salt; add to creamed mixture alternating with sour cream. Fold in apple and pear and pour mixture into prepared baking dish.

In the bowl of a food processor, combine brown sugar and cinnamon. Add cold butter slices and process until mixture resembles coarse crumbs. Stir in pecans and sprinkle topping mixture over batter.

Bake for 35 to 40 minutes or until a toothpick inserted near the center comes out clean. Cool on a wire rack.

Yield: 12 to 15 servings

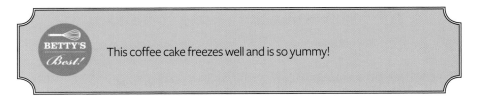

BETTY'S Best! This coffee cake freezes well and is so yummy!

TOMATO-HERB MINI FRITTATAS

12	large eggs
1½	cups half-and-half
½	teaspoon salt
¼	teaspoon freshly ground black pepper
2	tablespoons chopped fresh chives
1	tablespoon chopped fresh parsley
1	teaspoon chopped fresh oregano
1	pint grape tomatoes, halved
1½	cups shredded Italian three-cheese blend, divided

Preheat oven to 450 degrees. Lightly grease eight 4-inch (6-ounce) ramekins and place them on two baking sheets. Set aside.

In a blender or food processor, add eggs, half-and-half, salt and pepper and process until blended. In a small bowl, stir together chives, parsley and oregano.

In ramekins, layer tomatoes, one cup of cheese and chive mixture. Pour egg mixture over the top and sprinkle with remaining ½ cup cheese.

Place one baking sheet on middle oven rack and the second on the lower rack and bake for seven minutes. Switch baking sheets and bake seven to eight more minutes or until set. Remove top baking sheet from oven; transfer lower sheet to middle rack and bake an additional one to two minutes or until lightly browned.

Yield: 8 servings

PRALINE BACON

1	pound (12 slices) thick-sliced bacon
3	tablespoons sugar
1½	teaspoons chili powder
¼	cup finely chopped pecans

Preheat oven to 425 degrees.

Place bacon slices in a single layer on a broiler pan. Bake on the middle oven rack for 10 minutes or just until the bacon begins to turn golden brown. Meanwhile, in a small bowl, mix sugar and chili powder. Sprinkle bacon with sugar mixture and then with pecans. Return bacon to oven for five minutes longer or until brown and crisp.

Drain praline-side up on paper towels before serving.

Yield: 6 servings

Spice a dish with love and it pleases every palate.

FRENCH PROVERB

ITALIAN BREAKFAST COBBLER

Filling

1	pound bulk mild sausage
1	tablespoon vegetable oil
1	large onion, coarsely chopped
1	large red pepper, coarsely chopped
1	(8-ounce) package fresh whole mushrooms, sliced
2	(9-ounce) packages frozen chopped spinach, thawed and drained
2	cups shredded mozzarella or provolone cheese

Topping

1 ½	cups self-rising flour
½	cup grated Parmesan
1 ¼	cups milk
½	cup unsalted butter, melted
5	eggs, lightly beaten

Preheat oven to 400 degrees. Grease a 13×9-inch (3-quart) baking dish and set aside.

In a large skillet, cook sausage over medium-high heat for eight minutes or until browned. Remove with a slotted spoon and drain well.

Heat oil in the same skillet over medium-high heat until hot. Add onion and red pepper; cook five minutes. Add mushrooms and cook three more minutes or until vegetables are tender. Remove from heat. Stir in spinach and cooked sausage. Pour into prepared baking dish and sprinkle with shredded cheese.

In a medium bowl, combine all topping ingredients. Beat until smooth with a wire whisk. Pour over filling in baking dish.

Bake for 35 to 45 minutes or until golden brown.

Yield: 10 servings

HOT CURRIED FRUIT COMPOTE

1	large can sliced peaches		¾	cup brown sugar
1	small can apricots		4	teaspoons curry powder
1	large can sliced pears			
1	large can chunk pineapple			
10	red maraschino cherries			
⅓	cup unsalted butter, melted			

For best flavors, plan to prepare dish two days before serving.

Preheat oven to 325 degrees.

In a large baking dish, combine all ingredients and mix well. Cook for one hour, stirring occasionally. Cool and refrigerate for a full day. When ready to serve, warm fruit at 250 degrees for about 30 minutes or until warm through.

Yield: 10 servings

GEORGE'S CHOCOLATE BREAD PUDDING WITH SPICED CREAM

4	large eggs
1	cup firmly packed brown sugar
½	teaspoon ground cinnamon
⅛	teaspoon freshly grated nutmeg
1	teaspoon vanilla extract
1	cup semisweet chocolate chips, melted
¼	cup orange-flavored liqueur
2	cups half-and-half
8	Sister Schubert's® Dinner Yeast Rolls, broken into bite-sized pieces (4 cups)
2	cups semisweet chocolate chips
1	cup chopped pecans
	Spiced Cream

Preheat oven to 350 degrees. Butter a 6-cup loaf pan and set aside.

Whisk together eggs, sugar, cinnamon, nutmeg, vanilla, melted chocolate and orange-flavored liqueur until very smooth. Add half-and-half and mix well. Add bread pieces and let the mixture sit for 30 minutes, stirring occasionally.

Pour half the mixture into the prepared pan. Sprinkle top with half the unmelted chocolate chips and all the pecans. Pour in remaining bread mixture and top with remaining chocolate chips. Bake until pudding is set in the center, about 55 minutes. Cool for five minutes.

To serve, cut the pudding into 1-inch thick slices. Top with Spiced Cream.

Yield: 10 to 12 servings

. . . .

Spiced Cream

3	ounces cream cheese, softened
¼	cup sour cream
½	cup heavy cream, whipped
¼	cup sifted confectioners' sugar
¼ to ½ teaspoons cinnamon	

In a small bowl, stir together all ingredients until smooth. Spoon a large dollop of cream on top of Chocolate Bread Pudding to serve.

Bread is the warmest, kindest of words. Write it always with a capital letter, like your own name.

RUSSIAN PROVERB

HOLIDAY

Open House

The Christmas tree is trimmed, your home is gleaming with treasured decorations, and it is the perfect time for an Open House to offer greetings of the season to friends and relations. What an easy way to entertain a crowd; guests come and go within an established time, so there is plenty of time to visit while keeping trays filled and empty glasses whisked to the kitchen. Enlist the aid of a friend (or friends) to make sure that you have food and drink available at all times.

The menu was designed to include delicious nibbles that can be prepared ahead of time and will hold up for the duration of the party. This flexible menu can be used for any cocktail party or reception.

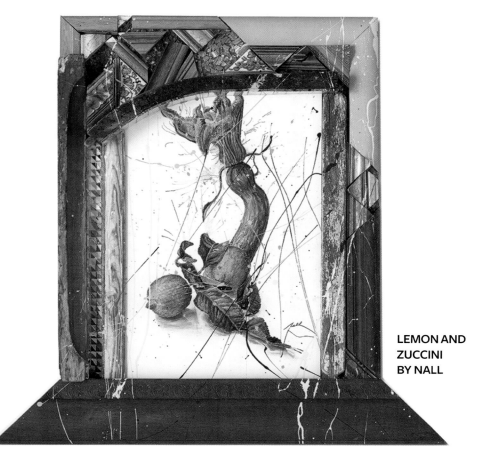

LEMON AND
ZUCCINI
BY NALL

MENU

Doc's Beef Tenderloin Sliders
with Maytag Blue Cheese Butter

Panko-Crusted Crab Cake Bites
with Roasted Pepper-Chive Aïoli

Chilled Asparagus with
Sesame-Ginger Vinaigrette

Baked Fiesta Spinach Dip

Warm Brie with Caramelized
Apples

Raspberry Chicken

Chocolate Orange Truffles

WINE SUGGESTION:
California Red and White Blend

DOC'S BEEF TENDERLOIN SLIDERS
WITH MAYTAG BLUE CHEESE BUTTER

1   (3- to 4-pound) fresh beef tenderloin, trimmed

3   garlic cloves, sliced

Sea salt and freshly ground black pepper to taste

4   slices bacon

½   cup unsalted butter, softened

2   tablespoons crumbled Maytag blue cheese

2   (10-ounce) bags Sister Schubert's® Dinner Yeast Rolls

Preheat oven to 425 degrees.

Season tenderloin with garlic, salt and pepper. Brown on all sides in a nonstick pan or seasoned iron skillet, turning to ensure even browning. Remove from oven and place in roasting pan with rack. Lay bacon strips over the meat.

Place in center of oven. Bake for 25 minutes for rare, 35 minutes for medium rare. If using a meat thermometer, refer to meat temperature chart on page 43.

Combine butter and blue cheese, stirring until well-blended. Spread a small amount evenly over sliced rolls and toast until lightly browned. Place tenderloin slices on bottom half of rolls and cover with top half. Assemble several hours before the party, toasting at the last minute.

BETTY'S Best!

A surgeon's tip from Doctor Bill. To trim or strip beef tenderloin, start with a sharp knife and remove extra fat. You also want to remove the "silver" connective tissue by starting on the small end of the tenderloin. If the end of the tenderloin is thin, fold it and secure with a toothpick to prevent over cooking.

PANKO-CRUSTED CRAB CAKE BITES
WITH ROASTED PEPPER-CHIVE AÏOLI

(These are easily assembled the night before and refrigerated. Remove from refrigerator an hour before baking.)

Crab Cakes

12	ounces shelled cooked crab
¼	cup finely diced celery
1	tablespoon minced chives
¼	cup mayonnaise
1	large egg, lightly beaten
1	teaspoon Dijon mustard
¼	teaspoon hot sauce
1 ¼	cups panko or fine dry bread crumbs, divided

Roasted Pepper-Chive Aïoli

Fresh chives, rinsed and cut into ¼-inch lengths

Preheat oven to 475 degrees. Grease a 12×17-inch baking pan and set aside.

Carefully pick crab and discard any bits of shell. In a large bowl, combine celery, minced chives, mayonnaise, egg, mustard and hot sauce; mix well with a fork. Fold in crab and ¼ cup panko and stir lightly just to blend.

Put remaining cup of panko in a shallow dish. Shape crab mixture into 24 cakes, each about 2 inches wide and ½ inch thick. Turn each cake in panko to coat well on all sides, pressing gently to make crumbs adhere.

Place cakes slightly apart on prepared baking pan and bake until golden brown, about 15 to 18 minutes. With a spatula, transfer crab cakes to a serving platter. Spoon a dollop of Roasted Pepper-Chive Aïoli on each cake and sprinkle with fresh chives. Serve hot.

Roasted Pepper-Chive Aïoli

⅓	cup mayonnaise
¼	cup drained and chopped roasted red pepper
1	tablespoon minced fresh chives
2	teaspoons lemon juice
1	teaspoon minced garlic

In the bowl of a food processor, pulse all ingredients until well blended. Can be made ahead and will keep for up to a week refrigerated in an airtight container.

A host is like a general; it takes a mishap to reveal his genius.

HORACE

CHILLED ASPARAGUS WITH
SESAME-GINGER VINAIGRETTE

3   pounds fresh asparagus spears

Salt to taste

Sesame-Ginger Vinaigrette

Snap off the woody ends of the asparagus and rinse well. Bring lightly salted water to a boil in a large pot. Add asparagus spears and cook for five minutes or just until tender-crisp. Drain asparagus and immediately plunge it into ice water to stop the cooking process. Pat asparagus dry and arrange on a serving platter. Drizzle the desired amount of Sesame-Ginger Vinaigrette evenly over asparagus. Serve immediately.

Yield: 10 servings

··

Sesame-Ginger Vinaigrette

3   tablespoons sesame seeds

3   small garlic cloves

1   tablespoon grated fresh ginger

¼   cup rice vinegar

¼   cup orange juice

4   teaspoons soy sauce

3   tablespoons vegetable oil

3   tablespoons sugar

¾   teaspoon red pepper flakes

½   cup sesame oil

Toast sesame seeds by placing them in a small skillet and heating over medium heat until fragrant and just golden in color, stirring frequently. Watch very carefully to prevent burning. Add sesame seeds and remaining ingredients to the jar of a blender and process until mixture is thoroughly combined and oils are incorporated. Refrigerate until ready to serve.

BETTY'S
Best!

If you want to take the time to do it, the ends of the asparagus which are usually discarded, make a nice stock. It can be frozen and used the next time you cook asparagus, or it may be used in place of any vegetable stock called for in a recipe!

BAKED FIESTA SPINACH DIP

1   tablespoon vegetable oil

1   cup chopped onion

1   cup chunky medium salsa, well drained

1   (10-ounce) package frozen chopped spinach, thawed and drained

2½   cups shredded Monterey Jack cheese, divided

1   (8-ounce) package light cream cheese, cubed

1   cup light cream

½   cup sliced black olives

1   cup chopped pecans

Preheat oven to 350 degrees. Lightly grease a 1 ½-quart baking dish and set aside.

Add oil to a large skillet and sauté onion over medium heat until tender. Stir in salsa. Add spinach that has been squeezed dry; cook for two minutes. Add two cups of cheese, cream cheese, cream and olives and blend well. Spoon mixture into prepared baking dish. Sprinkle with pecans and bake, uncovered, for 15 minutes or until hot through. Remove from oven and sprinkle with remaining cheese. Serve hot with pita chips or assorted crackers.

Yield: 5 cups

 BETTY'S *Best!* We actually suggest making this festive dip a day ahead, allowing the flavors to meld.

WARM BRIE WITH CARAMELIZED APPLES

¼   cup unsalted butter

4   large Golden Delicious apples, peeled, cored and sliced

¼   cup sugar

2   teaspoons cinnamon

1   (12-inch) wheel Brie cheese

1½   cups sliced almonds, toasted

Melt butter in a heavy skillet over medium-high heat. Sauté apples in butter for three minutes. Sprinkle with sugar and cinnamon and cook for eight more minutes or just until golden brown and tender, stirring frequently.

Slice cheese wheel in half horizontally. Spread half of the apple mixture over the bottom half of the cheese wheel. Top with remaining half of the cheese and spread remaining apple mixture over the top of that.

Place cheese wheel on a cardboard round. Microwave on high for 25 seconds. Place cheese, including cardboard round, on a serving tray. Sprinkle almonds over dish.

Serve with Bremner Wafers or your choice of cracker.

Yield: 50 cocktail servings

RASPBERRY CHICKEN

2	whole boneless, skinless chicken breasts, about two pounds
2	tablespoons butter
¼	cup chopped yellow onion
4	tablespoons raspberry vinegar
¼	cup chicken broth
¼	cup heavy cream
1	tablespoon canned crushed tomatoes
16	fresh raspberries, optional

Flatten each breast half by pressing it gently with the palm of your hand. Melt butter in a large skillet over medium heat. Raise heat slightly and add chicken pieces. Cook for about three minutes per side, or until they are lightly colored. Remove chicken from skillet and set aside.

Add onion to pan drippings and cook, covered, over low heat until tender, about 15 minutes. Add vinegar and increase heat. Cook, uncovered, stirring occasionally, until vinegar is reduced to about a tablespoon of syrup. Whisk in chicken broth, cream and tomatoes and simmer about one minute.

Return chicken to skillet and simmer gently in sauce, basting often, until it is just done and the sauce has been reduced and thickened slightly, about five minutes.

This may be made ahead to this point and refrigerated. Reheat and finish just before serving.

Remove chicken with a slotted spoon; cool and cut into bite-sized chunks. Add raspberries to sauce in the skillet and cook over low heat for one minute. Do not stir berries with a utensil; simply swirl them by moving the skillet. Pour sauce over chicken and transfer to a chafing dish. Serve immediately in pastry cups.

Yield: 10 to 12 cocktail servings

BETTY'S Best! This delicious chicken recipe was on the menu for my daughter Lisa's wedding reception served as a hot hors d'oeuvres. It presents beautifully and is always a favorite.

CHOCOLATE ORANGE TRUFFLES

¼	cup unsweetened butter, chopped
⅓	cup heavy cream
7	ounces semisweet chocolate chips
1	egg yolk
1	teaspoon grated orange zest
2	tablespoons orange-flavored liqueur
	Finely chopped pecans

Add butter, cream and chocolate chips to a 1-quart glass measuring cup. Microwave on medium power for two minutes. Remove from microwave and whisk until smooth. Quickly whisk in egg yolk; add orange zest and orange liqueur. Chill until firm.

Add pecans to a shallow dish. Roll chocolate mixture into 1-inch balls and roll each one in pecans, pressing gently to make them adhere.

Yield: about 20 truffles

NOTE: Truffles can be frozen. Remove from freezer to thaw just in time to serve.

RINGING IT IN

New Year's Bash

Open your home to your friends for a lively salute to the New Year with this delectable upscale menu for a crowd, or choose a mellow "Just Desserts" soirée instead. Decorate your home with fresh greenery and plenty of candlelight, and check out your local party shop for paper hats, noisemakers, and confetti. Rearrange furniture to feature seating areas for conversation, and find the perfect mix of background music for the festivities. You will have time to enjoy your party because most of the menu is prepared ahead. Polish the serving trays and prepare attractive garnishes for drinks and trays. One bottle of Champagne serves five people, so make sure you have enough chilled Champagne for toasting through the evening.

Raise your glass to a joyful new beginning!

MENU

Pulled Pork on Sister's
Dinner Yeast Rolls

Jan's Olive Spread

Hot Crab Crisps

Feta Black Bean Dip

Smoked Salmon Mousse
on Endive

Meatballs in Peanut Curry Sauce

Sweet and Salty Chocolate-
Bacon Fudge

SUGGESTED WINE:

Red Zinfandel from the Lodi
Region of California

Freixenet Champagne

**Nall and Muffin
enjoying a holiday
open house**

PULLED PORK ON SISTER'S DINNER YEAST ROLLS

1 (5- to 6-pound) bone-in pork butt

1½ teaspoons kosher or coarse salt

¾ teaspoon black pepper

3 cups beef broth

1 tablespoon liquid smoke
seasoning

2 (10-count) bags Sister
Schubert's® Dinner Yeast Rolls

Caper Mustard Sauce (page 70)

Red Onion Marmalade (page 70)

Preheat oven to 350 degrees. Place pork butt in a large pot or Dutch oven with a lid. Season with salt and pepper. Pour broth around pork until it covers about one-quarter of the meat. Stir in liquid smoke seasoning. Cover pot and place in oven. Bake pork until internal temperature registers 190-200 degrees on an instant-read thermometer and meat is falling apart, about 3 ½ to 4 ½ hours. Use a fork to test pork to be sure it comes apart easily. Remove pork from oven and let it sit in pot for about 15 to 20 minutes.

Remove from pot and discard bone and cooking liquid. Cut fatty parts off meat and then use two forks or your fingers to shred meat into small pieces. Place "pulled" pork in a large bowl. This much may be done a day ahead of the party and then reheated when ready to use.

Warm rolls according to package directions. Split and spread bottoms with Caper Mustard Sauce. Pile pork onto rolls. Top with Red Onion Marmalade and top with other half of roll. Another option is to plate pork on rolls and serve sauces on the side.

Yields: 20 small sandwiches

CAPER MUSTARD SAUCE

1 ½ cups mayonnaise

½ cup sour cream

1 small jar capers, drained

3 tablespoons white wine

2 tablespoons Dijon mustard

½ teaspoon white pepper

Combine all ingredients for sauce in a glass bowl and mix well. Cover with plastic wrap and chill until ready for use.

· ·

Red Onion Marmalade

2 large red onions, thinly sliced

3 tablespoons brown sugar

¾ cup dry red wine

3 tablespoons balsamic vinegar

Salt and black pepper to taste

In a large saucepan, combine onions and sugar; cook over moderate heat, stirring often, until onions begin to soften and caramelize, about 15 minutes.

Stir in wine and vinegar, increase heat to moderate high and bring to a boil. Reduce heat to low and cook, stirring often, until most of the liquid has evaporated, about 15 more minutes. Season to taste with salt and pepper. Cool, cover and refrigerate up to three weeks; serve at room temperature.

Yield: 2 cups

Sister and Betty teaching and enjoying each other's company during one of their dual cooking classes at Betty's.

JAN'S OLIVE SPREAD

1 cup drained and sliced pimiento-stuffed green olives

1 cup drained and sliced seedless black olives

1 bunch green onions, chopped

1 cup mayonnaise

1 cup grated sharp Cheddar cheese

1 cup grated Monterey Jack cheese

Dash of Tabasco sauce

Combine all ingredients and mix well. Cover and chill. Can be made ahead. Best if used within 3 days.

Serve with wheat crackers, crostini or scoops.

Yield: approximately 4 ½ cups

HOT CRAB CRISPS

2 baguettes, thinly sliced

½ cup finely chopped green onion

1 cup freshly shredded Parmesan

4 drops Tabasco sauce

1 tablespoon fresh lemon juice

1 cup mayonnaise

8 ounces fresh crabmeat, picked for shells

Preheat oven to 300 degrees. Spread baguette slices on a baking sheet lined with parchment or nonstick foil and crisp in oven for about 10 minutes.

In a medium mixing bowl, combine green onion, Parmesan, Tabasco and lemon juice; toss lightly. Stir in mayonnaise and blend well. Carefully fold in crabmeat.

Increase oven temperature to 350 degrees. Spread crab mixture on baguette rounds and bake for 15 minutes or until bubbly and lightly browned. Serve immediately.

Yield: 50 to 55 rounds

To cook well, one must love and respect food.

CRAIG CLAIBORNE

FETA BLACK BEAN DIP

½ cup sugar

¾ cup apple cider vinegar

¾ cup vegetable oil

2 (15-ounce) cans black beans, drained and rinsed

2 (15-ounce) cans shoe peg corn, drained and rinsed

1 bunch scallions, chopped

¾ cup cilantro, chopped

1 (8-ounce) block feta cheese, crumbled

In a large bowl, whisk together sugar, vinegar and vegetable oil until well blended. Add black beans, corn, scallions, cilantro and feta and mix well. Cover and chill until serving time. Can be made the day before. Serve with tortilla chips or corn chips.

Yield: About 8 cups

BETTY'S Best! Leftovers are good served over lettuce as a salad.

SMOKED SALMON MOUSSE ON ENDIVE

¼ pound smoked salmon

2 dashes Tabasco sauce

2 dashes Worcestershire sauce

Freshly ground white pepper to taste

½ cup heavy cream

24 endive leaves, trimmed and separated

Place salmon, Tabasco, Worcestershire and white pepper in the bowl of a food processor. Process until smooth.

In a medium bowl, whip cream until it holds stiff peaks. Gently fold into salmon mixture. Chill. When ready to serve, pipe or spoon mousse into prepared endive leaves.

Yield: 24 servings

KRISTY HYDE'S IMAGINATIVE MURAL GRACES THE STAIRWELL WALL DESCENDING TO BETTY'S COOKING SCHOOL, OFFERING STUDENTS A UNIQUE BEGINNING TO THEIR CULINARY EXPERIENCE.

MEATBALLS IN PEANUT CURRY SAUCE

½ cup all-purpose flour

1 pound medium-lean ground beef

1½ teaspoons salt

¼ teaspoon freshly ground black pepper

2 tablespoons canola oil

4 garlic cloves, coarsely chopped

1 tablespoon red curry paste

1 cup canned coconut milk (thicker part of milk)

2 tablespoons chunky peanut butter

2 teaspoons fish sauce

1½ tablespoons sugar

1 teaspoon chopped mint for garnish

Put flour into a large ziptop bag. Place ground beef in a bowl and sprinkle with salt and pepper and mix well. Shape into 1-inch balls. Place meatballs in bag, a few at a time. Shake to coat meatballs and shake off excess.

Line a plate with paper towels and set aside. Heat oil in skillet over medium heat. Add garlic and fry for two minutes. Watch carefully to prevent burning. After cooking time, remove garlic with a slotted spoon and set aside.

Increase heat to high and add meatballs. Sear until evenly browned, about four minutes. Add more oil as needed during frying. Again using a slotted spoon, transfer meatballs to the paper-lined plate.

Add red curry paste to remaining oil in skillet and cook for two minutes, stirring with a wooden spoon. This releases the aroma and taste of the red curry. Add reserved garlic, coconut milk and peanut butter. Cook and stir until smooth. Add fish sauce and sugar; taste and adjust seasonings as needed. Return meatballs to the pan and coat with sauce. Garnish with mint before serving.

Yield: 24 (1-inch) meatballs

SWEET AND SALTY CHOCOLATE-BACON FUDGE

1   pound bacon

2   cups chopped pecans

4   (4-ounce) semisweet chocolate baking bars, chopped

1   (14-ounce) can sweetened condensed milk

¼   cup unsweetened butter, softened

⅓   cup heavy cream

In a large skillet, cook bacon over medium-high heat until crisp; remove bacon and drain on paper towels.

In a medium nonstick skillet, heat pecans over medium-low heat, stirring often, for six to eight minutes or until toasted and fragrant. Watch closely to prevent burning. Line an 8-inch square baking pan with aluminum foil. Spray foil with nonstick cooking spray.

In a medium saucepan, combine chocolate, condensed milk, butter and cream. Cook over medium-low heat, stirring constantly, until chocolate melts and mixture is smooth. Remove from heat.

Crumble bacon, reserving ¼ cup. Stir pecans and remaining bacon into chocolate mixture. Spoon mixture into prepared pan; smooth top with a spatula. Sprinkle reserved ¼ cup of crumbled bacon over chocolate mixture, pressing gently to adhere. Cover and chill at least four hours or until set. Cut into squares to serve.

Yield: Approximately 24 pieces

Love feels like chocolate wrapped in bacon.

ANONYMOUS

NEW YEAR'S

Black-Eyed Pea Day

Southern tradition holds that one must eat black-eyed peas on New Year's Day in order to ensure good luck in the coming year. Some folks go a step farther and say that you must eat your peas under the table. We can't vouch for that, but you can double your chances for good luck with two great black-eyed pea recipes! Turnip greens are considered an acquired taste, but once you master the technique for cooking greens our way, you may become a convert. And there is no such thing as turnip greens without cornbread, period. So pick out some dark fresh leafy greens, rinse them until you think all the sand is gone, then rinse them again to be sure. And dig into these iconic Southern dishes. Don't let those in the know have all the good luck!

MENU

Gracie's New Year's Dip with
Tomato Conserve

Chutney-Almond Cheese Spread

Hoppin' John Salad

George's Meatloaf

Harry's Bar Macaroni and
Cheese

Turnip Greens with Honey
Nall Style

Key Lime Pie Vicki with Rum
Chantilly Cream

SISTER Says!

Begin your New Year with lots of luck! Southern tradition calls for eating black-eyed peas on New Year's Day for good luck. I've enjoyed serving Gracie's New Year's Dip for several years. I met Gracie and her son Frank Foster at the Gourmet Food Show in Atlanta, and we became instant friends for life. Like Betty and me, Frank and I share a love of family, friends, and food! This dip served with Gracie's Tomato Conserve is truly a real Southern treat! This is my version of her Tomato Conserve. Simply drizzle the conserve over the top of this dip and enjoy the luck that you and yours deserve.

GRACIE'S NEW YEAR'S DIP WITH TOMATO CONSERVE

2	(8-ounce) packages cream cheese, softened
½	cup mayonnaise
½	cup finely chopped green onion
1	tablespoon Worcestershire sauce
2	cups shredded extra-sharp Cheddar cheese
½	cup bacon bits
2	cans black-eyed peas, drained

Tomato Conserve

Preheat oven to 375 degrees. Lightly grease a 1 ½-quart baking dish and set aside.

Combine all ingredients in a large mixing bowl and stir well. Spoon mixture into prepared dish and cook until hot through and bubbly, about 20 minutes. Remove from oven and cool for five minutes. Drizzle top with Tomato Conserve and serve with scoop-style corn chips, crackers or crusty bread.

Yield: 4 cups

NOTE: Sour cream may be substituted for the mayonnaise in this recipe. Also, if you want to cook your own peas, you will need about 2 ½ cups.

Tomato Conserve

¼	cup water
2	cups chopped tomatoes, puréed
1 ½	cups chopped apples, puréed
6	tablespoons light brown sugar
2	tablespoons lemon juice
¼	teaspoon salt
¼	teaspoon pectin

In a medium, heavy saucepan, bring water, puréed tomatoes and apples to a boil. Add remaining ingredients and cook on medium until the sugar is dissolved and conserve begins to thicken, about 20 to 25 minutes. Remove from heat. Cool and refrigerate; use within two weeks.

Yield: 1 quart

CHUTNEY-ALMOND CHEESE SPREAD

2 (8-ounce) packages cream cheese, softened

2 cups grated sharp Cheddar cheese

6 tablespoons sherry

2 tablespoons Worcestershire sauce

1 ½ teaspoons curry powder

½ teaspoon salt

1 (8-ounce) jar Major Grey's Chutney

¾ cup almonds, toasted and coarsely chopped

½ cup thinly sliced green onion

½ cup flaked coconut

Combine cream cheese, Cheddar, sherry, Worcestershire, curry powder and salt until well blended. Spoon into a bowl or decorative mold that has been lined with plastic wrap. Wrap well with additional plastic wrap or aluminum foil and refrigerate several hours or overnight.

When ready to serve, unmold and spread with chutney. Press chopped almonds on top and sprinkle with a layer of green onion and coconut. Serve at room temperature with crostini or assorted crackers.

Yield: 20 or more cocktail servings

HOPPIN' JOHN SALAD

This recipe can be doubled easily.

½ cup uncooked long-grain rice

¼ cup fresh lemon juice

¼ cup olive oil

1 jalapeño pepper, seeded and minced

1 garlic clove, minced

1 teaspoon salt

¼ teaspoon pepper

1 (15-ounce) can seasoned black-eyed peas, drained and rinsed

½ cup finely chopped celery

½ cup loosely packed fresh parsley leaves, chopped

¼ cup chopped green onion

Prepare rice according to package directions and set aside.

In a large bowl, whisk together lemon juice, olive oil, jalapeño pepper, garlic, salt and pepper. Stir in rice, peas, celery and parsley until blended. Cover and chill two hours. Sprinkle with green onion immediately before serving.

Yield: 6 servings

GEORGE'S MEATLOAF

3	cups soft bread cubes (about 4 slices)
¾	cup milk
2	eggs, lightly beaten
1 ½	pounds ground beef
½	pound ground pork
¼	cup finely chopped onion
¼	cup finely chopped celery
1	tablespoon Worcestershire sauce
1 ½	teaspoons salt
⅛	teaspoon pepper
½	teaspoon poultry seasoning
1	cup ketchup
½	cup white corn syrup

Preheat oven to 350 degrees.

Soak bread cubes in milk. Add eggs and beat slightly. Add meats, onion, celery, Worcestershire sauce, salt, pepper and poultry seasoning. Mix well with hands but do not overwork the mixture. Form into two loaves and place them in a 13×9×2-inch baking pan lined with foil.

Bake, uncovered, for one hour.

For glaze, mix together ketchup and white corn syrup until well blended. Spread glaze over the loaves and return to oven for an additional 15 minutes.

Yield: 8 to 10 servings

Sister and George relishing a rare quiet moment together.

HARRY'S BAR MACARONI AND CHEESE

1 (12-ounce) package wide egg noodles

2 cups heavy cream

2½ cups whole milk

2 teaspoons all-purpose flour

½ teaspoon salt

¼ teaspoon freshly ground black pepper

2 cups packed grated Fontina cheese, divided

¾ cup packed finely grated Parmesan, divided

¾ cup packed grated mozzarella, divided

4 ounces cooked ham, diced, optional

2 tablespoons finely chopped fresh Italian parsley

Preheat oven to 450 degrees. Butter a 13×9-inch glass baking dish and set aside.

Cook noodles in a large pot of salted water until al dente, stirring frequently, about 5 minutes. Drain well but do not rinse.

In a large bowl, whisk together cream, milk, flour, salt and pepper until well blended. Stir in one cup Fontina, ½ cup Parmesan, ½ cup mozzarella, ham (if using) and parsley. Add noodles and toss to coat.

Transfer noodle mixture to prepared baking dish. In a small bowl, toss together remaining cheeses to blend. Sprinkle cheese mixture over noodle mixture.

Bake until sauce bubbles and cheese melts and begins to brown on top, about 20 minutes. Let stand 10 minutes before serving.

Yield: 12 to 15 servings

TURNIP GREENS WITH HONEY NALL STYLE

2 large bunches fresh turnip greens

½ pound lean salt pork, cut into 1-inch strips

4 tablespoons bacon drippings

3 tablespoons raw honey

½ cup olive oil

Salt and pepper to taste

Wash greens to remove dirt and sand; rinse at least three times, using plenty of cold, fresh water. Put any small leaves directly into a large heavy pot. Strip larger leaves from stems before adding them.

Add pork strips and bacon drippings to greens and pour in one quart cold water. Cover pot and bring to a boil. Stir greens and press down so they will be covered by water.

Lower heat and simmer for at least two hours—the longer the better. Add water as needed to keep greens covered. Cook to desired tenderness.

Remove from heat, add honey and stir. Just before serving, drizzle olive oil over top of greens. Season with salt and pepper to taste. Serve hot.

NOTE: The liquid accumulated from cooking greens, known in the south as "potlikker," is delicious served over cornbread and splashed with a little hot pepper sauce.

KEY LIME PIE VICKI WITH RUM CHANTILLY CREAM

Vicki is our friend who runs a cooking school in Destin, Florida, where we teach when time allows. A perfect ending to a wonderful menu—light and refreshing.

3	eggs, separated
1	can sweetened condensed milk
⅓	cup key lime juice
1	(9-inch) pre-baked pie shell

Preheat oven to 250 degrees.

With a hand mixer, whip egg whites until soft and fluffy (not stiff peaks) and set aside. Whip egg yolks and add sweetened condensed milk. Stir in key lime juice and whip until filling is well mixed. Gently fold reserved egg whites into mixture and pour into baked pie shell. Bake for 15 minutes. Let stand to cool, and then refrigerate to chill.

Rum Chantilly Cream:

1	cup heavy cream
1	tablespoon vanilla bean paste
1	tablespoon light rum
2	tablespoons confectioners' sugar

Using a hand mixer, whip cream, adding vanilla bean paste. Gradually add rum and sugar. Spoon over chilled pie before serving.

NOTE: If it is available in your area, we recommend using Floribbean Organic Key Lime Juice. It has no additives and the taste is so fresh! Additionally, pure vanilla extract may be substituted for the vanilla bean paste.

Sister and Betty during one of their first cooking classes together at Kitchenique. Vicki can be seen in the background, always working hard to make sure the chefs have everything they need.

VALENTINE'S
Sweetheart Dinner

Would you be my Valentine?

Even though we no longer decorate shoe boxes and exchange handmade Valentines with friends, we still love that sweet question. These days we favor a beautiful bouquet of roses, a sweet card, and a romantic dinner date at home with our favorite beau.

The time, effort, and love you put into preparing these scrumptious dishes will show your sweetheart that he is your Valentine for always!

VILLE DE NANTES CAMELLIA BY NALL

PEAR AND BLUE CHEESE SALAD
WITH BLACKBERRY BALSAMIC DRESSING

Salad

12   cups assorted greens

1   cup crumbled blue cheese

4   pears, cored and sliced

1   cup salted almonds, toasted

Add greens, cheese, pears and almonds to a large salad bowl. Pour dressing over greens to serve.

Dressing

½   cup balsamic vinegar

3   tablespoons Dijon mustard

½   cup blackberry preserves

2   garlic cloves, minced

½   teaspoon salt

¼   teaspoon pepper

1   cup olive oil

Whisk together vinegar, mustard, preserves, garlic, salt and pepper in a bowl until well mixed. Add olive oil in a fine stream, whisking until completely incorporated.

Yield: 12 servings

SMOKED SAUSAGE IN PUFF PASTRY

1   sheet puff pastry

6   smoked sausages

1   egg

2   tablespoons water

     Dip for Sausage Pastry

Preheat oven to 400 degrees. Thaw puff pastry according to package directions. Line a baking sheet with parchment and set aside.

Sauté sausages in a large skillet over medium heat for about 10 minutes or until cooked through. Remove from heat and cool.

Roll puff pastry into a rectangle and cut into six equal pieces. Wrap pastry around each of the sausages. In a small bowl, lightly beat egg with water. Brush each pastry with the egg wash and place on prepared baking sheet.

Bake for 15 minutes or until lightly browned. Cut each into three slices and serve with dip.

Yield: 18 pieces

. . . .

Dip for Sausage Pastry

2   cups seedless plum or raspberry marmalade

1   tablespoon prepared horseradish

1   tablespoon Worcestershire sauce

¼   cup cider vinegar

1   teaspoon ground cinnamon

1   teaspoon vanilla extract

Combine all ingredients in a medium mixing bowl and blend well. Spoon into a small decorative bowl for serving.

Yield: about 2 ½ cups

Cooking is like love. It should be entered into with abandon or not at all.

HARRIET VAN HORNE

PROVENCAL LAMB

1   (6- to 7-pound) bone-in leg of lamb, trimmed and tied

½   cup Dijon mustard

3   tablespoons chopped garlic (9 cloves), divided

1   tablespoon fresh rosemary leaves

1   tablespoon balsamic vinegar

Kosher salt and finely ground black pepper

½   cup quality olive oil

½   cup quality liquid honey, divided

1   large Spanish onion, sliced

4   sprigs fresh thyme

2   sprigs fresh rosemary

Preheat oven to 450 degrees.

Place leg of lamb in a large roasting pan, fat side up, and pat dry with paper towels. Combine mustard, one tablespoon garlic, rosemary, vinegar, 1 tablespoon salt and ½ teaspoon pepper in a mini food processor and pulse until garlic and rosemary are minced. Spread mixture on lamb.

Place olive oil, ¼ cup honey, onion, remaining two tablespoons garlic, two tablespoons salt and two teaspoons pepper in a bowl and toss well. Pour the mixture around the lamb and tuck in thyme and rosemary sprigs. Drizzle lamb with remaining ¼ cup honey.

Roast 20 minutes. Lower heat to 350 degrees and roast another 1 to 1 ¼ hours, or until a meat thermometer registers 130 to 135 degrees for medium-rare. Place the lamb on a cutting board, cover with foil, and allow to rest 15 minutes. Discard herb stems. Slice lamb, arrange on a platter and sprinkle with salt and pepper. Spoon pan juices over lamb slices and serve immediately.

Yield: 8 to 10 servings

....

PANKO-BATTERED FRIED ASPARAGUS

4   eggs, lightly beaten

1   cup milk

2   cups all-purpose flour

4   cups panko bread crumbs

    Seasoned salt and pepper to taste

2   pounds fresh asparagus, washed and trimmed

Canola oil for frying

In a dish long enough to accommodate the asparagus spears, mix eggs and milk. In another comparable dish, add flour, panko, salt and pepper and mix well.

Dip asparagus spears in egg mixture and then roll in crumb mixture.

Heat oil in a large skillet and fry asparagus in small batches. Drain on paper towels before serving.

Yield: 8 to 10 servings

ORANGE CARROTS

24	small, young carrots
6	tablespoons unsalted butter
⅔	cup brown sugar
	Juice of 4 oranges
¼	teaspoon ground nutmeg
¼	teaspoon ground cinnamon
4	slices unpeeled oranges

Wash and scrape or peel carrots. Heat butter in a large skillet or saucepan with a lid. Add sugar, orange juice and spices. Cook for three minutes, stirring constantly. Add carrots. Spoon syrup over them, cover with orange slices and cook, partially covered, until carrots are tender and liquid has almost cooked away. Baste often, returning lid to pan each time.

Yield: 12 servings

Bill and Betty Sims enjoying dinner and conversation with friends.

The way to a man's heart is through his stomach.

MRS. SARAH PAYSON PARTON

FLOURLESS CHOCOLATE-ORANGE ALMOND CAKE

1 ½ cups whole almonds

1 cup sugar, divided

6 ounces bittersweet or semisweet baking chocolate, coarsely chopped

½ cup unsweetened cocoa powder

½ cup orange juice

2 teaspoons grated orange zest

6 large eggs, separated

1 vanilla bean, split lengthwise

¼ teaspoon salt

Preheat oven to 350 degrees. Spray a heart-shaped (or round) springform pan with nonstick spray that includes flour. Blend almonds and ¼ cup sugar in a food processor until almonds are finely ground. Add chocolate; blend until chocolate is finely ground, scraping sides and bottom of bowl occasionally.

Whisk together cocoa, orange juice and orange zest in a small bowl until smooth. Combine egg yolks and ½ cup plus two tablespoons sugar in large bowl. Scrape in seeds from vanilla bean. Using an electric mixer, beat until yolk mixture is very thick, about four minutes. Beat in cocoa mixture. Fold in ground almond mixture.

Add egg whites to a large mixing bowl and, using clean, dry beaters, beat egg whites and salt until soft peaks form. Gradually add two tablespoons sugar, beating until whites are stiff but not dry. Fold whites into chocolate batter in three additions. Transfer to prepared pan.

Bake cake until tester inserted into center comes out clean, about 40 minutes. Cool cake completely in pan on a wire rack. Run a sharp knife around cake while it is in the pan; release sides. Cut cake into wedges to serve.

NOTE: This cake may be made a day ahead of serving. Cover it loosely with foil and store it at room temperature.

If you don't have a heart-shaped pan and use a round one, you can simply decorate it for the holiday. Draw a heart-shaped pattern on a piece of cardboard that is large enough to cover the top of the cooled cake. Cut the heart out of the center, place remaining cardboard over the cake and dust it with confectioner's sugar. Lift the cardboard and you have a lovely white heart on the cake!

CHOCOLATE CORDIAL CUPS FILLED WITH LEMON CURD
(page 208)

AN
Elegant Easter

R ich in Christian tradition, Easter is also wonderful fun for both the Barnes family and the Sims family. Easter Egg Hunts figure in the fun for both.

Sister and George host an annual Easter Egg Hunt for their St. Mary's church family the day before Easter, complete with live bunnies for photo-ops. Springtime in South Alabama needs no additional decoration, and the stately house and grounds display an abundance of blossoming shrubs along with tulips, daffodils, Japanese Magnolia, azaleas, and roses. Sweeping lawns provide more than enough space for a multitude of little ones, and the Easter Bunny has plenty of help in Sister's kitchen. The family dinner on Sunday is more formal, marked by peaceful joy in celebration of shared Christian faith and hope.

CHERRIES JUBILEE-BLACK PEPPER
GLAZED HAM AND MARY HOLLIS'
SWEET POTATO ORANGE CUPS

PENCIL CAMELLIA
BY NALL

MENU

Sweet Fruit Iced Tea

Smoked Salmon on Crostini
with Dill Sauce

Goat Cheese Walnut Tassies

Cherries Jubilee-Black Pepper
Glazed Ham

Elegant Potatoes
OR
Mary Hollis' Sweet
Potato Orange Cups

Iceberg Lettuce Wedge with
Blue Cheese Dressing

Asparagus in the Pink

Sister Schubert's®
Parker House Style Rolls

Ambrosia

Sister's Lemon Strawberry/
Blueberry Trifle

SWEET FRUIT ICED TEA

1 ½   cups water

4   cups sugar

6   cups pineapple juice

4   cups orange juice

1   cup lemon juice

½   gallon weak tea

1   large bottle ginger ale

Fresh mint sprigs

Add water and sugar to a medium saucepan. Heat until sugar is dissolved. Cool and add to juices and tea. Immediately before serving, add cold ginger ale. Serve over ice in tall iced tea glasses and garnish with fresh mint.

TIPS FOR THE PERFECT BOILED EGG

If you want to center the yolk when preparing hard-cooked eggs, here is an easy tip. Twenty-four hours before cooking, wrap two rubber bands around the egg carton to hold it shut. Then lay it on its side in the refrigerator. When you cook the eggs, the yolks will be perfectly centered.

Hard-cooked eggs are much easier to peel if you put them in a bowl of ice water for several minutes. The eggs literally shrink away from the shell's interior, making peeling a breeze.

To prevent the shells from cracking, add a pinch of salt to the water before hard-cooking eggs.

HOLIDAY CELEBRATIONS

CHERRIES JUBILEE-BLACK PEPPER GLAZED HAM

1   (10- to 12-pound) smoked,
     ready-to-cook bone-in ham

1   (14-ounce) can low-sodium
     chicken broth

1¼   cups cherry preserves (about two
     12-ounce jars)

¾   cup brandy

¼   cup cider vinegar

1   tablespoon freshly ground black
     pepper

3   tablespoons whole grain Dijon
     mustard

3   tablespoons cane syrup

Fresh cherries for garnish

Fresh sage sprigs for garnish

Preheat oven to 275 degrees. Remove skin from ham and trim fat to about ¼-inch thickness. Make shallow cuts in fat one inch apart in a diamond pattern. Place ham in a foil-lined roasting pan. Add broth to pan.

Stir together preserves, brandy, vinegar, pepper, mustard and cane syrup in a heavy saucepan; bring to a boil over medium-high heat, stirring constantly. Reduce heat to medium-low; simmer, stirring constantly for five minutes or until mixture is slightly reduced. Remove half of cherry mixture to a small bowl. Cover and refrigerate until serving time. Brush ham with remaining cherry mixture.

Bake ham on lower rack of oven for 4 to 4½ hours or until a meat thermometer inserted into thickest portion registers 148 degrees, basting with cherry mixture every 30 minutes. Ham should rest 15 minutes before slicing to serve.

If desired, heat reserved chilled cherry mixture and serve with ham along with additional Dijon mustard. Garnish with fresh cherries and fresh sage sprigs to serve.

Yield: 10 servings

MARY HOLLIS' SWEET POTATO ORANGE CUPS

6   sweet potatoes, unpeeled
     and washed

½   stick butter, softened

¼   cup orange juice

¼   cup chopped pecans

6 or 7 large navel oranges, washed

1   (16-ounce) bag mini
     marshmallows

Preheat oven to 375 degrees.

In a large pot, cover sweet potatoes with cold water, bring to a boil and cook until fork tender. Drain and let cool slightly before peeling potatoes. In a large bowl, mash potatoes until smooth. Stir in butter, orange juice and pecans and mix well.

For the orange shells, cut each orange in half and scoop out the pulp using a small knife or grapefruit spoon. Reserve the pulp for Sister's Ambrosia (page 99), salads or fresh juice.

Fill each orange shell with the potato mixture and top with marshmallows. Bake until hot and the marshmallows are melted.

ASPARAGUS IN THE PINK

3 pounds fresh asparagus, trimmed

3 cups mayonnaise

1 cup roasted red peppers, drained

½ teaspoon cayenne pepper

Cook asparagus in boiling water to cover for seven minutes (slightly less for thinner stalks). Drain in a colander and cover immediately with ice. Let stand until cool and drain on paper towels.

Combine mayonnaise, red peppers and cayenne pepper in a food processor and process for one minute. Sauce may be prepared up to 3 days ahead. Keep refrigerated in an airtight container.with

 BETTY'S *Best!*

For a stunning presentation, spoon sauce into a brandy snifter or decorative crystal glass and place it in the center of a silver or crystal tray. Arrange some of the asparagus spears with bottoms in sauce and tips flaring out the top of the container. Arrange remaining asparagus spears in a spoke pattern around the base of the snifter.

In the childhood memories of every good cook, there is a large kitchen, a warm stove, a simmering pot and a mom.

BARBARA COSTIKYAN

GOAT CHEESE WALNUT TASSIES

1 cup fresh bread crumbs

1 cup finely ground walnut pieces

2 tablespoons melted unsalted butter

1 teaspoon salt, divided

1 teaspoon freshly ground black pepper, divided

1 (8-ounce) package cream cheese, softened

10 ounces goat cheese (Montrachet), softened

2 large eggs, lightly beaten

2 tablespoons chopped fresh chives

Walnut halves for topping

2 teaspoons finely diced red bell pepper

Preheat oven to 350 degrees. Butter or spray three mini muffin pans and set aside.

In a medium bowl, combine bread crumbs, ground walnuts, butter, ½ teaspoon salt and ½ teaspoon pepper; stir until thoroughly combined. Spoon a rounded teaspoon of walnut mixture into each cup and press down to the bottom of the cups, forming a crust.

With an electric mixer, beat cream cheese until light and fluffy. Add goat cheese and beat until creamy. Add eggs and beat until well combined. Stir in chives and the remaining ½ teaspoon salt and pepper. Spoon goat cheese mixture into the crumb-lined cups; lightly smooth tops.

Garnish half of the tassies with a walnut half lightly pressed into the top. On remaining tassies, spoon a small amount of the diced red pepper on the top.

Bake until puffed and lightly browned, about 12 to 15 minutes. Cool pans on wire racks for 5 minutes and then carefully remove tassies to a serving plate.

Yield: 12 servings

TASSIE CUPS WITH WARM SHRIMP AND ARTICHOKES (page 201)

SMOKED SALMON ON CROSTINI WITH DILL SAUCE

8	ounces smoked salmon
30	crostini (recipe follows)

Dill Sauce

1 ½	cups mayonnaise
1	cup sour cream
2	tablespoons dried or 3 tablespoons freshly chopped dill

Salt and pepper to taste

Combine mayonnaise, sour cream and dill and mix well. Add salt and pepper to taste.

To assemble, place a small rolled piece of salmon on each crostini. Garnish with a small dollop of Dill Sauce or pipe the sauce on with a decorator tube.

Crostini

1	package Sister Schubert's® Dinner Yeast Rolls
1	cup unsalted butter, melted
1	cup olive oil
1	teaspoon minced garlic
3	tablespoons mixed chopped fresh dill, chives, thyme and dried parsley flakes

Allow rolls to thaw completely.

Combine butter, olive oil, garlic and herbs in a bowl and mix. Slice rolls vertically into ¼-inch slices.

Preheat oven to 220 degrees. Cover a baking sheet with foil or parchment. Using a pastry brush, brush each side of the bread slices with the butter mixture and arrange on prepared baking sheet. Bake for one hour or until crisp. Cool on a wire rack.

If not using crostini immediately, seal them in an airtight container or ziptop bag.

BETTY'S Best! These crostini freeze beautifully and do not have to be reheated before using. Just thaw uncovered and serve. I keep a bag in my freezer at all times.

ICEBERG LETTUCE WEDGE WITH BLUE CHEESE DRESSING

2 heads iceberg lettuce

2 cups grape tomatoes, halved

4 hard-cooked eggs, chopped

8 slices bacon, fried and crumbled

Blue cheese crumbles for garnish

Blue Cheese Dressing

Sister's Homemade Croutons (page 97)

Cut lettuce heads in half and rinse well in cold water. Place on a clean tea towel to drain. Cut lettuce halves into quarters and remove core. Place each wedge on an individual chilled serving plate or a large platter. Top each with a sprinkle of tomato and chopped egg. Garnish with bacon crumbles and cheese crumbles. Add Blue Cheese Dressing and Sister's Homemade Croutons to serve.

Yield: 8 servings

Blue Cheese Dressing

8 ounces reduced-fat cream cheese, softened

½ cup reduced-fat mayonnaise

½ cup (2 ounces) crumbled blue cheese

1 teaspoon Worcestershire sauce

2 tablespoons low-fat milk

⅛ teaspoon pepper

In the bowl of a food processor, add cream cheese, mayonnaise, blue cheese, Worcestershire, milk and pepper. Pulse to break any large pieces of the blue cheese.

Serve immediately or chill in an airtight container for up to one week.

Yield: 8 servings

 SISTER *Says!* Gorgonzola is just as good as the blue cheese crumbled on this salad. But what you don't want to change is adding my homemade croutons!

SISTER'S HOMEMADE CROUTONS

1   package Sister Schubert's® Dinner Yeast Rolls

4   tablespoons unsalted butter

6   tablespoons (3 ounces) extra-virgin olive oil

3   tablespoons fresh or dried coarsely chopped rosemary

2   garlic cloves, minced

Allow rolls to thaw completely. Preheat oven to 325 degrees.

Cut rolls into cubes, ½- to 1-inch size, depending on your choice. Place cubes in a large bowl.

Melt butter and combine with olive oil, rosemary and garlic. Pour mixture over bread cubes and toss well to coat each one. Spread cubes on baking sheets, making sure they do not touch. Bake for 20 to 30 minutes or until golden and crispy.

 SISTER Says! These make a great addition to any soup or salad. You may substitute any of your favorite herbs for the rosemary. Try basil, oregano, or thyme for a nice variety.

ELEGANT POTATOES

2   pounds small unpeeled red potatoes

⅓   cup unsalted butter

1   cup sliced green onions

     Salt and pepper to taste

2   cups sour cream

6   slices crisply fried bacon, drained and crumbled

2   cups shredded sharp Cheddar cheese

Cook potatoes in enough water to cover in a saucepan just until tender; drain. Let stand until cool. Slice potatoes and set aside.

Preheat oven to 350 degrees. Spray a 3-quart baking dish with cooking spray and set aside.

Melt butter in a small skillet and sauté green onions until just tender-crisp. In the prepared dish, layer half of the potato slices, salt, pepper, sour cream, green onion, bacon and cheese. Repeat layers, ending with cheese. Bake for 20 minutes or until hot in the center and golden brown on top.

Yield: 8 to 10 servings

SISTER'S LEMON STRAWBERRY/BLUEBERRY TRIFLE

2   pints fresh blueberries, washed and sorted

2   pints fresh strawberries, washed, hulled and diced

⅔   cup sugar, divided

Juice of 1 lemon

1   tablespoon grated lemon zest

2   teaspoons cornstarch

1   quart heavy cream

½   teaspoon almond extract

1   (11-ounce) jar lemon curd

1   pan Sister Schubert's® Parker House Style Rolls, prepared according to package

Combine berries in a large bowl; sprinkle with ⅓ cup sugar, lemon juice, lemon zest and cornstarch. Transfer mixture to a large saucepan and, over medium heat, simmer berry mixture until berries begin to soften and release juice, approximately three minutes. Set aside to cool.

Using the large bowl of mixer on high speed, whip cream with ⅓ cup sugar and almond extract until soft peaks form. Do not overbeat. Using a small bowl, combine a tablespoon of lemon curd with 2 tablespoons of whipping cream, stirring until well combined. Add remaining lemon curd and combine with whipping cream. Beat on high speed until somewhat stiffer peaks form and lemon curd is well incorporated.

Remove rolls from pan and cut into 1-inch pieces.

To assemble trifle, spoon a layer of whipped cream filling into a large glass trifle bowl. Add a layer of rolls. Add a layer of berries with juice. Continue layering until all rolls and berries have been used. Finish with a layer of lemon filling.

Cover tightly with plastic wrap and refrigerate until ready to serve.

Yield: 12 to 15 servings

AMBROSIA

10   navel oranges, peeled and segmented

6   grapefruit (pink or white), peeled and segmented

1   (15.5-ounce) can crushed pineapple, with syrup

¾   cup sugar

¼   cup Cointreau or amaretto

1   cup grated sweetened coconut

Combine all ingredients except coconut and refrigerate at least four hours or overnight. Serve in fruit cups and sprinkle with coconut.

SISTER Says! We always had to leave the coconut off my father's ambrosia, as he didn't care for it. And my grandmother would top each of the children's servings with a maraschino cherry. Yum!

Holiday Celebrations

MOTHER'S DAY

Luncheon

OR BRUNCH

"We celebrated Mother's Day by having dinner for my two wonderful aunts, Maggie and Dinks, along with Grandmother and Granddad on my mother's side of the family, who lived on the street behind us. Today our family gathers together; the husbands, sons, and daughters pitch in and let the 'moms' sit back and relax. Spending time together is the best gift of all." *Betty*

"Both of my grandfathers passed away before I was born, but I was blessed to know and love my Great Grandmother Dorothy, Grandmother Satchie (both from Louisiana), and Grandmother Leona (Alabama). All were outstanding cooks, with different expertise, and I learned so much from each of them. It keeps their memory alive in my life by sharing their wonderful recipes and techniques with you! Every Mother's Day at home my sisters and I wore a red or pink flower to church, to signify that our mother was alive. A white flower meant that one's mother had passed away. Thankfully, I can still wear a red rosebud for my sweet Mama." *Sister*

COLD DILLED SQUASH SOUP

MENU

Demitasse of Cold Dilled Squash
Soup with Bacon Cheese Toasts

Avocado Mousse
with Shrimp Salad

Assorted Fresh Fruits
and Melon Balls

Sister Schubert's®
Parker House Style Rolls

Strawberry Tiramisu

2	**small leeks**
1 ½	**pounds yellow squash**
2	**tablespoons vegetable oil**
3	**cups chicken broth**
1	**cup half-and-half**
1	**(8-ounce) container sour cream**
½	**teaspoon salt**
2	**tablespoons minced fresh dill**
	Fresh dill sprigs, for garnish

Split leeks lengthwise and wash well under running water to remove the dirt from between leaves; slice. Wash squash and cut into ½-inch-thick rounds. In a Dutch oven over medium-high heat, sauté leeks in oil until tender. Add squash and broth. Bring to a boil; reduce heat and cover. Simmer 8 to 10 minutes or until squash is tender. Remove from heat and cool. Purée with immersion blender or pulse in blender.

Return mixture to Dutch oven and add half-and-half, sour cream, salt and dill. Whisk mixture until blended and smooth. Place mixture in refrigerator to chill thoroughly before serving.

Ladle into bowls or demitasses. Garnish with dill sprigs and serve.

Yield: 6 to 8 servings or 16 demitasse servings

BACON CHEESE TOASTS

1	**loaf sliced white sandwich bread**
1	**cup grated Swiss cheese**
8	**slices bacon, crisply fried and crumbled**
4	**tablespoons mayonnaise**
1	**tablespoon finely grated onion**
½	**teaspoon celery salt**

Remove crusts from bread. Place bread slices on a large baking sheet. Preheat oven to 325 degrees.

In a small mixing bowl, combine cheese, bacon, mayonnaise, onion and celery salt and mix well. Spread mixture evenly on bread slices. Bake for 10 minutes.

Cool and, using a small sharp knife, cut bread slices into rectangles, triangles or other shapes of choice.

Yield: 12 servings

NOTE: Don't discard the bread crusts. Toss them in a freezer bag and use them for bread crumbs or croutons later.

AVOCADO MOUSSE WITH SHRIMP SALAD

2   cups mashed ripe avocado

1   (8-ounce) package cream cheese, softened

1   cup mayonnaise

2   tablespoons unflavored gelatin

4   tablespoons cold water

1   (3-ounce) package lime-flavored gelatin

1   (3-ounce) package lemon-flavored gelatin

3 ½   cups hot water

Boston lettuce leaves

Shrimp Salad

Place avocado, cream cheese and mayonnaise in the bowl of a food processor and process until smooth. Set aside.

Dissolve unflavored gelatin in cold water; dissolve flavored gelatins in hot water. Stir unflavored gelatin into flavored gelatins and mix well. Place mixture in refrigerator and let set until partially congealed. At that point, blend in reserved avocado mixture and mix thoroughly.

Oil an 8-cup gelatin mold and spoon mousse mixture into it. Lightly smooth the top and refrigerate until completely set. When ready to serve, dip mold in warm water to loosen and turn out onto a decorative plate or platter lined with Boston lettuce leaves. Fill center of the ring with Shrimp Salad before serving.

Serve with assorted melon balls and fresh fruit.

....

Shrimp Salad

1   pound large shrimp

4   quarts water

1   (3-ounce) package of seafood-boil seasoning

½   cup mayonnaise

½   cup sour cream

1   can sliced black olives, drained

1   tablespoon fresh dill

½   cup finely chopped celery

⅓   cup chopped green onion

2   tablespoons lemon juice

Cayenne to taste

Peel and devein shrimp. In a large pot, add water and seafood-boil seasoning and bring to a rolling boil. Add shrimp and reduce heat. Cook for 3 minutes. Remove from heat, leaving shrimp in the water until they are pink and firm to the touch. Drain shrimp and chop into bite-sized chunks.

Mix shrimp with remaining ingredients, cover and refrigerate at least two hours, or overnight. Spoon salad into center of Avocado Mousse to serve.

Yield: 16 servings

SISTER *Says!* George is the shrimp cooker in our family and for good reason. He has perfected his shrimp. He says to make sure your water and seasoning are at a rolling boil before adding the shrimp. Three minutes is the perfect cook time for large shrimp.

STRAWBERRY TIRAMISU

1 ½ cups strawberry preserves

⅓ cup plus 4 tablespoons orange liqueur, divided

⅓ cup orange juice

1 pound mascarpone cheese, room temperature

1 ½ cups chilled heavy cream

⅓ cup sugar

2 teaspoons vanilla extract

1 ½ pounds fresh strawberries, divided

52 (approximately) ladyfingers

Whisk preserves, ⅓ cup orange liqueur and orange juice in a 2-cup measuring cup.

Place mascarpone cheese and two tablespoons orange liqueur in a large bowl; fold ingredients just to blend.

In another large bowl, using an electric mixer, beat cream, sugar, vanilla and remaining two tablespoons orange liqueur to just soft peaks. Stir about a quarter of whipped cream mixture into mascarpone mixture to lighten; fold in remaining whipped cream mixture.

Hull and slice half the strawberries. Spread ½ cup preserve mixture over bottom of a 3-quart oblong serving dish or a 13×9×2-inch glass baking dish. Arrange enough ladyfingers over preserve mixture to cover bottom of the dish. Spoon ¾ cup preserve mixture over ladyfingers, then spread 2 ½ cups mascarpone mixture over them. Arrange sliced strawberries over mascarpone layer. Repeat layering with remaining ladyfingers, preserve mixture and mascarpone mixture. Cover with plastic wrap and chill at least 8 hours or overnight.

Slice remaining strawberries. Arrange over tiramisu and serve.

NOTE: Soft ladyfingers are traditionally used for making tiramisu. However, if they are not available, crispy ones may be used.

Any congealed salad with cream cheese or sour cream will melt if you try to loosen in warm water before unmolding. Instead use very dry fingers to pull sides away from the mold, then flip it over on a serving plate for a perfect result.

CHOOSE YOUR TEAM!

Super Bowl Sunday

CELEBRATION WITH FRIENDS

After months of Sunday night football and Monday night football and the playoffs, it is finally time for—are you ready—the Super Bowl!

Football fans are ready to crown a new champion and non-fans are just ready for it all to disappear. Either way, it's a wonderful excuse for a party. Super Bowl entertaining is the ultimate casual event. Phone or email your friends, wear your favorite jeans, and chill the beer. Our menu is guaranteed to please your guests all the way from kickoff to overtime!

"MAM MOMMY'S" PEYTON MANNING FAN

PARTY ANTIPASTO TRAY

½ medium-size head iceberg lettuce

1 small head curly endive

1 (3.5-ounce) package thinly sliced pepperoni

1 (4-ounce) package thinly sliced Genoa salami, quartered

1 (6-ounce) package thinly sliced Italian ham

1 (11.5-ounce) jar pepperoncini, drained

1 (2-ounce) can anchovies with capers, drained

1 (15-ounce) can garbanzo beans, drained

1 pint cherry tomatoes

1 cup radishes

½ cup ripe olives

½ cup green olives

8 ounces provolone cheese, cubed

¼ cups Antipasto Dressing

Shred lettuce and spread on a large tray. Make a border of endive leaves around the edge of the tray. Arrange meats, vegetables, olives and cheese on top of shredded lettuce. Serve with Antipasto Dressing.

Yield: 10 to 12 servings

··

Antipasto Dressing:

¾ cup olive or vegetable oil

¼ cup white wine vinegar

1 tablespoon dried oregano

1 teaspoon dried basil

¼ teaspoon dried thyme

⅛ teaspoon pepper

2 tablespoons water

1 garlic clove, crushed

Combine all ingredients in a screw-top jar. Cover tightly and shake vigorously. Let stand several hours at room temperature.

Yield: 1 ¼ cups

MENU

Party Antipasto Tray

Salted Almonds

Warm Spinach Salad with Balsamic Raspberry Syrup

Shrimp Jambalaya

Sister Schubert's® Parker House Style Rolls

Sister's Sweet Potato Pie

Cinnamon Chocolate Brownies with Chocolate Ganache

SUGGESTED BEVERAGES:

Spanish Rioja Red Wine and assorted craft beer

WARM SPINACH SALAD
WITH BALSAMIC RASPBERRY SYRUP

3	cups balsamic vinegar
1	cup Raspberry Coulis (see recipe)
6	cups fresh spinach, cleaned and stemmed

Salt and pepper to taste

1	cup fresh raspberries
1	cup fresh blueberries
4	ounces feta

In a medium saucepan over high heat, reduce balsamic vinegar by ⅔ or until syrup consistency, about 20 minutes. Add raspberry coulis and bring sauce up to a simmer. Remove from heat.

Add spinach to a large salad bowl and season with salt and pepper. Toss with Balsamic Raspberry Syrup and plate on salad plates. Sprinkle top of salads with fresh berries and feta. If serving salad from a bowl, add berries and feta after tossing.

Yield: 8 to 10 servings

RASPBERRY COULIS

1	cup fresh raspberries
½	cup sugar

Place berries and sugar in a food processor and pulse until smooth.

SHRIMP JAMBALAYA

8	strips of bacon
2	medium onions, chopped
1	cup chopped celery
1	large green pepper, chopped
1	cup uncooked rice
2	cups beef broth, heated
1	ounce hot sauce
1	ounce Worcestershire sauce
1	bay leaf
	Black pepper to taste
	Seasoned salt to taste
1	pound raw shrimp, peeled and deveined

In a large stockpot, fry bacon. Remove bacon and set aside. Sauté onions, celery and pepper in ¼ inch of bacon drippings. Add rice and brown slightly. Add broth that has been heated to boiling; stir in all other ingredients except shrimp and bacon. Cook until rice is tender. Add shrimp and continue cooking until shrimp is done, about 10 minutes. Do not overcook shrimp. Remove from heat, crumble bacon on top and serve.

Yield: 8 servings

BETTY'S Best! A Sims family favorite that has an amazing flavor.

SUPER BOWL SHOPPING

Be flexible when planning a menu, and be sure it can be easily executed by you. Calculate how much food to buy and then shop early.

SISTER'S SWEET POTATO PIE

2 pounds sweet potatoes, peeled and sliced

½ cup unsalted butter

3 large eggs

1 cup sugar

½ cup sweetened condensed milk

½ cup evaporated milk

1 teaspoon ground nutmeg

1 teaspoon vanilla extract

Grated zest of 1 orange

2 (9-inch) Flaky Pie Crusts (page 35)

Cook sweet potatoes in boiling water to cover for 30 minutes or until tender when pierced with a fork. Drain well.

Preheat oven to 350 degrees.

Beat sweet potatoes and butter at medium speed with an electric mixer until smooth. Add eggs, sugar, milks, nutmeg, vanilla and orange zest and beat well. Pour mixture evenly into the two pie crusts. Bake on lower rack of oven for 45 to 50 minutes or until set. Garnish, if desired, with whipped cream.

Yield: 2 (9-inch) pies

SISTER *Says!* A tip about sweet potatoes…Mamie, my nanny, taught me to look for sweet potatoes with a smooth surface as they are less likely to be stringy. Also, the "Red Jewel" sweet potatoes are very sweet.

CINNAMON CHOCOLATE BROWNIES
WITH CHOCOLATE GANACHE

Brownies

½   cup all-purpose flour

1 ½   teaspoons cinnamon

½   teaspoon salt

6   (1-ounce) squares semisweet chocolate, chopped

1 ½   sticks unsalted butter, chopped and softened

4   large eggs

1   cup sugar

1 ½   teaspoons vanilla extract

1   cup chopped walnuts

Preheat oven to 350 degrees. Butter and lightly flour an 8×8-inch metal baking pan and set aside.

In a small bowl, combine flour, cinnamon and salt and mix well. Add semisweet chocolate and butter to a 2-quart glass measuring cup and microwave on high for two minutes. Stir mixture and microwave on half power until chocolate has melted, about two more minutes. Whisk until smooth.

Beat eggs and sugar in a large mixing bowl for five minutes or until mixture thickens and falls in soft ribbons when beaters are lifted. Beat in vanilla. Stir in flour mixture, half at a time, blending well after both additions. Add warm chocolate mixture gradually, beating until just combined. Fold in walnuts and spoon mixture into prepared pan.

Position a rack in the center of the oven and bake brownies for 35 minutes or until the top is set and a tester inserted in the center comes out with moist crumbs attached. Do not over bake. Cool completely in the pan, on a wire rack. Pour Chocolate Ganache over cooled brownies.

Chocolate Ganache

2   cups semisweet chocolate chips

1   cup heavy cream

Add chocolate chips to a 2-quart glass measuring cup and microwave for two minutes. Stir and return to microwave in 30-second intervals to complete melting. When chips are melted, add heavy cream and whisk until mixture is smooth and glossy. Pour evenly over smoothed brownies. Cover with plastic wrap and chill for two hours or until ganache is set. Cut into squares to serve.

Yield: 16 medium squares

A PORCH PARTY AT SEASIDE

Memorial Day

Although initially established to honor those who lost their lives in the Civil War, after World War I, Memorial Day became an annual day of remembering those who gave their lives in all wars involving the United States.

It was first known as Decoration Day, when cities and towns across the country would "decorate" their homes and streets, as well as military cemeteries, with flags and flowers to remind everyone of those lost. We now see it as a day to celebrate their sacrifices and along with friends and family, we gather under flags and bunting to share food and memories…and to create new memories as well.

Our menu honors the colors and the season of Memorial Day. Lots of fresh fruits and vegetables weigh down tables on porches and patios nationwide, and ours are no exception. Vegetable spread and vegetable lasagna, succotash and salads are all easy to prepare and share the plate with fresh shrimp and garlic bread. Mint brownies and lemon-glazed pound cake are a cool completion to this traditional first day of summer. The calendar may not confirm it, but we all know in our hearts that the hot days are coming soon and the memories stirred by Memorial Day will linger as long as those summer days.

MENU

Strawberry Margaritas

Tea Punch

Snappy Vegetable Spread

Shrimp Cocktail Ring

Noel's Special Pimiento Cheese

Catherine's Vegetable Lasagna

Green Salad with Mint

Butter Bean and Corn Succotash

Garlic Bread

Chocolate Mint Brownies

Lemon Cream Cheese
Pound Cake

Every Memorial Day the Sims, Brandon and Stainback families gather at the Stainbacks' Seaside home for a Porch Party. This family tradition now includes three generations and is enjoyed by all ages.

STRAWBERRY MARGARITAS

1   **basket ripe strawberries (about 12)**

1   **cup tequila**

1   **tablespoon confectioners' sugar**

    Juice of 1 lime

1   **tablespoon strawberry syrup**

    Crushed ice

Clean and hull strawberries. Add all ingredients in a blender with the crushed ice. Blend and serve immediately.

Yield: 6 servings

SNAPPY VEGETABLE SPREAD

2	tomatoes, cut into small dice
1	cup finely diced celery
1	small onion, finely diced
1	red pepper, finely diced
1	cucumber, finely diced
1	teaspoon salt, divided
1	envelope unflavored gelatin
¼	cup cold water
¼	cup boiling water
1	pint mayonnaise

Line a large colander with several thicknesses of paper toweling. Add all chopped vegetables to the colander and sprinkle with ¼ teaspoon salt to help vegetables release moisture.

Soften gelatin in cold water and stir in boiling water. Fold in mayonnaise and remaining salt. Add well-drained vegetables and mix well. Cover and refrigerate until serving time.

Use as a spread for crackers, crostini or bread.

Yield: 20 appetizer servings

TEA PUNCH

2   family-size tea bags

2   cups sugar

1   (12-ounce) can frozen orange juice concentrate

1   (12-ounce) can frozen lemonade concentrate

Crushed ice

Fresh mint sprigs for garnish

Brew tea according to package directions. Pour into a one-gallon container.

Add sugar, orange juice concentrate, lemonade concentrate and enough water to fill the container. Stir well and serve over crushed ice, garnished with mint sprigs.

Yield: 1 gallon

NOTE: If you have saved the liquid when draining canned fruits such as pears, peaches, pineapple, or apricots, you may use that to replace some or all of the water needed for this punch.

Paul, Isabelle, Lisa, Laurie, and Sherri

Raspberries are best not washed. After all, one must have faith in something.

ANN BATCHELDER

NOEL'S SPECIAL PIMIENTO CHEESE

2   **red bell peppers**

2   **cups grated extra-sharp white Cheddar**

2   **cups grated extra-sharp yellow Cheddar**

4   **ounces cream cheese, softened**

½   **cup homemade mayonnaise (or Duke's)**

Freshly ground black pepper to taste

4 to 5 dashes of Tabasco

Quarter and seed peppers. Place them, skin side up, on a foil-lined baking sheet. Broil for 9 to 10 minutes or until skin is totally black. Pull foil up around peppers making a tightly sealed bag, allowing peppers to steam. When peppers are cool enough to handle, peel and discard the blackened skin. Dice the roasted flesh into medium dice. Set aside.

In a large bowl, mix cheeses, mayonnaise, black pepper and Tabasco with a mixer. A food processor may be used, taking care to not over blend. Add diced peppers and stir well but do not process.

Chill and serve with assorted crackers or on sliders.

Yield: 4 cups

NOTE: You may also purchase jarred roasted peppers if you don't have time to do your own. They are usually found near the pickles at the supermarket.

SISTER *Says!*   I add ¼ cup grated onion, using large holes on a box grater, and 1 tablespoon of Worcestershire sauce to give the spread a little kick.

GREEN SALAD WITH MINT

2	tablespoons balsamic vinegar or white wine vinegar
2	tablespoons fresh lemon juice
6	tablespoons extra-virgin olive oil
6	tablespoons honey
18	cups mixed baby greens
½	cup pine nuts
1	cup fresh mint leaves, loosely packed

Coarse salt and freshly ground black pepper

In a large salad bowl, whisk together vinegar and lemon juice. Add olive oil in a slow, steady stream, whisking constantly until incorporated. Whisk in honey.

Add greens, pine nuts, mint, salt and pepper and toss well to coat greens.

Yield: 10 servings

SHRIMP COCKTAIL RING

3 pounds jumbo shrimp, peeled and deveined, tails intact

Cocktail Sauce

2 cups ketchup

¼ to ⅓ cup prepared horseradish

1 tablespoon fresh lemon juice

1 ½ teaspoons Worcestershire sauce

Fill a 5 ½ cup ring mold with water and freeze overnight.

In a large pot, boil salted water. Reduce heat to low and add shrimp, cooking until they turn pink, about four to five minutes. Drain and refrigerate to chill.

Turn mold upside down and quickly run it under hot water. Invert onto a serving platter and return to freezer for two hours.

Meanwhile, stir together ketchup, horseradish, lemon juice and Worcestershire sauce to make Cocktail Sauce. Blend all ingredients well and spoon into a serving bowl that will fit inside the ice ring.

When ready to serve, place bowl in the ring and add shrimp over the edges atop the ice.

Yield: 12 servings

CATHERINE'S VEGETABLE LASAGNA

Marinara Sauce

¼ cup extra-virgin olive oil

1 small onion, peeled and finely chopped

2 garlic cloves

1 celery stalk, finely chopped

1 carrot, peeled and finely chopped

1 (32-ounce) can crushed tomatoes

2 teaspoons dried basil

3 dried bay leaves

1 teaspoon sea salt

1 teaspoon black pepper

In a large skillet, heat olive oil; add onion and garlic and sauté for 10 minutes. Add celery and carrot and continue cooking another 10 minutes, stirring frequently. Add tomatoes, basil, bay leaves, salt and pepper. Cook uncovered over low heat for about an hour or until sauce reaches desired consistency. Remove bay leaves and discard.

Noodles

2 tablespoons vegetable oil

1 teaspoon salt

1 (8-ounce) package lasagna noodles

Bring a large pot of water to a boil; add vegetable oil and salt. Add lasagna noodles and cook to al dente, about four minutes. Drain and rinse. Carefully place noodles on a baking sheet and cover with a damp tea towel to prevent pasta from drying out. Set aside.

Vegetable Filling

2 (10-ounce) packages frozen chopped spinach, thawed

3 tablespoons olive oil

1 large zucchini, finely chopped

1 large summer squash, finely chopped

1 cup sliced mushrooms

½ teaspoon salt

½ teaspoon black pepper

Squeeze excess moisture from spinach, making it as dry as possible. Heat olive oil in a large skillet. Add spinach, squash and mushrooms; sauté for five minutes, then season with salt and pepper.

Cheese Filling and Topping

½ cup freshly grated Parmesan

2 cups ricotta cheese

4 tablespoons chopped fresh parsley or 2 tablespoons dried parsley

2 eggs, lightly beaten

1 teaspoon salt

½ teaspoon black pepper

1 (8-ounce) package fresh mozzarella, sliced, for topping

Add all cheese filling ingredients, except the mozzarella, to a large bowl and mix until well blended.

To assemble

Preheat oven to 375 degrees. Lightly grease a 9×13-inch baking dish.

Spoon one-third of marinara sauce into the prepared dish and spread evenly over the bottom. Layer in half the noodles and cover with half the vegetable filling, then half the cheese filling. Repeat layers and spread top with remaining one-third of marinara sauce. Add mozzarella slices as a single layer on top.

Bake uncovered until bubbly and hot through, about 20 minutes.

NOTE: Baking this dish too long could result in the cheese becoming tough.

BUTTER BEAN AND CORN SUCCOTASH

8 cups water

2 tablespoons salt

2 cups fresh or thawed frozen butter beans (limas)

2 tablespoons unsalted butter

1 small sweet onion, finely diced

1 garlic clove, minced

2 cups uncooked corn kernels, fresh or frozen

½ cup chicken broth

½ cup heavy cream

Salt and freshly ground black pepper

Chopped fresh parsley for garnish

Bring water and salt to a rolling boil. Add butter beans and cook until tender on medium, about 20 to 30 minutes. Drain and immediately immerse into ice water to stop the cooking process and to preserve the bright green color.

Melt butter in a medium saucepan over medium heat. Add onion and garlic and cook about one minute. Stir in corn, broth and cream. Toss in butter beans and season to taste with salt and pepper.

Sprinkle with chopped fresh parsley and serve hot.

Yield: 8 to 10 servings

CHOCOLATE MINT
BROWNIES

GARLIC BREAD

2	Sister Schubert Baguettes
6	garlic cloves, finely minced
¼	cup minced fresh parsley
2	tablespoons minced fresh basil
1	teaspoon pepper
½	cup olive oil
¼	cup unsalted butter, softened
½	cup grated Parmesan

Preheat oven to 375 degrees. Slice baguettes down the center and place them on a large parchment-lined baking sheet.

In a small bowl, stir together garlic, parsley, basil, pepper, olive oil and butter. Mix well and spread down the center of each split baguette. Sprinkle with Parmesan and bake 15 to 20 minutes.

Yield: 20 slices

CHOCOLATE MINT BROWNIES

Brownies

8	ounces unsweetened chocolate
1	cup unsalted butter
1	cup regular margarine
4	cups sugar
8	eggs, lightly beaten
2	cups all-purpose flour
1	teaspoon salt

Preheat oven to 350 degrees. Coat an 11×13-inch baking pan with nonstick spray and set aside.

Combine chocolate, butter and margarine in a two-quart microwave-safe dish. Microwave at half power until melted, stirring at two-minute intervals. Combine sugar and eggs in a large mixing bowl and mix well. Stir in chocolate mixture, flour and salt. Stir to blend but do not over work the batter. Spoon mixture into prepared pan and bake for 30 minutes. Remove from oven and cool.

Filling

1	cup unsalted butter, softened
4	cups sifted confectioners' sugar
½	teaspoon green food coloring
2	teaspoons mint flavoring

With an electric mixer, beat butter and sugar until well blended. Add coloring and mint flavoring. Blend well and spread over cooled brownie. Chill before icing.

Chocolate Icing

3	cups chocolate chips
1 ½	cups heavy cream

Microwave chocolate chips on medium power in a two-quart glass measuring cup for two minutes or until melted. Add heavy cream, whisking until smooth. Spoon icing over the top of the filling. Refrigerate. Cut into squares to serve.

Yield: 48 small squares

Betty with daughter Libby.

LEMON CREAM CHEESE POUND CAKE

1½ cups unsalted butter, softened

1 (8-ounce) package cream cheese, softened

3 cups sugar

6 large eggs

3 cups all-purpose flour

¼ teaspoon salt

1 teaspoon vanilla extract

1 tablespoon lemon extract

1 tablespoon almond extract

Lemon Glaze

Preheat oven to 325 degrees. Spray a 12-cup Bundt pan or tube pan with nonstick cooking spray with flour. Set aside.

In a large bowl, combine butter, cream cheese and sugar. Beat at medium speed with an electric mixer until fluffy. Add eggs, one at a time, beating well after each addition.

In a medium bowl, sift together flour and salt. Gradually add flour mixture to butter mixture, beating until combined. Add extracts, beating to blend. Spoon batter into prepared pan.

Bake until a wooden pick inserted near the center of the cake comes out clean, about 1 hour and 30 minutes. Let cake cool in pan for 30 minutes. Remove from pan and let cool completely on wire rack. Drizzle with Lemon Glaze.

Lemon Glaze

2 cups confectioners' sugar

¼ cup fresh lemon juice

In a small bowl, whisk together sugar and lemon juice until smooth. Spoon glaze over top and down sides of the cake.

All-American Celebrations

A PATRIOTIC CELEBRATION ON THE SOUND

4th of July

When our forefathers signed the Declaration of Independence on July 4, 1776, they gave America her birthday, and a birthday this significant deserves a celebration! There are never enough flags and bunting to suit us, but there is always plenty of great food and drink.

Who needs a birthday cake when we have the wonderful Southern staple, home-made tea cakes! Served with fresh strawberries, blueberries, and whipped cream, they take their place among the best desserts in the land. And although you might think they are too pretty to eat, you will surely be missing out if you don't try one of Chrissie's 4th of July cookies. Sister's daughter Chrissie is a master baker, whose treats are both beautiful and delicious.

So light the sparklers, wave the flag, and eat, drink, and be patriotic!

MENU

White Sangria

Hot Corn Dip

Charlotte's Tri-Color Orzo Salad

German Potato Salad

Butter Bean Salad

Oven-Roasted Barbequed Brisket
Sliders with Sauerkraut Slaw
or
Greg's Barbequed Baby Back Ribs

Sister's Tea Cakes with
Strawberries and Blueberries

Chrissie's Sugar Cookies

WHITE SANGRIA

WHITE SANGRIA

1   bottle dry white wine

Juice of 1 lemon

2   tablespoons sugar

1   peach, sliced

1   lemon, sliced

1   orange, sliced

1   (7-ounce) bottle lemon-lime soda

Mix all ingredients except soda together in a two-quart thermos or pitcher. When ready to serve, add soda, stir and pour into ice-filled glasses. Be sure everyone gets pieces of fruit.

Yield: 6 to 8 servings

HOT CORN DIP

1	**cup unsalted butter**
2	**(8-ounce) packages cream cheese**
¼	**cup milk**
4	**(12-ounce) cans corn kernels with peppers, drained**
1	**(6-ounce) jar pickled jalapeño chiles, drained**
6	**ounces shredded Cheddar cheese**

Preheat oven to 315 degrees. Grease a two-quart baking dish and set aside.

Melt butter and cream cheese in a saucepan with milk, stirring frequently. Stir in corn and jalapeño chiles. Fold in cheese. Spoon mixture into prepared dish and bake for 30 minutes. Serve with scoop-style corn chips.

Yield: 15 to 20 servings

BUTTER BEAN SALAD

1   pound baby lima beans

1   red onion, minced

1   cup mayonnaise

2   teaspoons grated white horseradish

1   teaspoon Worcestershire sauce

2   tablespoons lemon juice

½   teaspoon salt

Dash of Tabasco sauce

1   teaspoon crumbled fresh rosemary

3   slices bacon, crisply fried and crumbled

In a medium saucepan, cover lima beans with water and cook until beans are tender. Drain and rinse under cold water. Spoon beans into a large serving bowl.

Combine onion, mayonnaise, horseradish, Worcestershire sauce, lemon juice, salt, Tabasco, rosemary and bacon in a small bowl; mix well.

Pour over lima beans, stirring gently to coat. Chill, covered, until serving time. Fresh or frozen limas will work for this recipe.

Yield: 6 servings

BETTY'S *Best!*

"Butter beans," the colloquial name for baby green limas, are highly prized in the South. When perfectly cooked, the inside of the bean becomes creamy and takes on a rich, buttery texture. This recipe goes well in many different menus.

CHARLOTTE'S TRI-COLOR ORZO SALAD

¼ cup red wine vinegar

2 tablespoons fresh lemon juice

1 tablespoon honey

½ cup olive oil

Salt and pepper to taste

6 cups chicken broth

1 (1-pound) package tri-color orzo

2 cups red and yellow teardrop or grape tomatoes, halved

1 (7-ounce) package feta cheese, cut into ½-inch cubes

1 cup chopped fresh basil

1 cup chopped green onion

½ cup toasted pine nuts

Whisk together vinegar, lemon juice and honey in a small bowl. Gradually whisk in oil. Season vinaigrette with salt and pepper. Dressing may be made two days ahead of serving, covered and refrigerated.

Bring broth to a boil in a large heavy saucepan. Stir in orzo, reduce heat to medium and cover partially. Boil until orzo is tender but still firm to the bite, stirring occasionally. Drain well.

Transfer orzo to a large salad bowl, tossing frequently to cool. Add tomatoes, feta, basil and green onion to orzo. Pour in vinaigrette and toss well to coat. Season with salt and pepper.

This may be made two hours ahead of serving and left to stand at room temperature. Add pine nuts and toss immediately before serving at room temperature.

Yield: 8 to 10 servings

SISTER Says!

My daughter Charlotte lives in Miami, where there is never a "bad weekend" for getting together with friends!

This is always on the menu and has become one of my favorite salads to serve as well.

Charlotte says to be very careful when toasting the pine nuts. If you over cook them they develop an unpleasant taste. Less is better with these—just a light brown is best.

*All that I am in life,
I owe to my mother.*

PRESIDENT ABRAHAM LINCOLN

GERMAN POTATO SALAD

8	large potatoes
1	pound bacon, cut into 1-inch pieces
2	medium onions, peeled and chopped
¾	cup brown sugar, firmly packed
½	cup white vinegar
¼	cup all-purpose flour
2	cups water
½	teaspoon salt

Boil potatoes until tender in lightly salted water. Drain, cool and slice potatoes. Place potatoes in a 9×12-inch baking dish and set aside.

Fry bacon and onions in a large skillet until bacon is brown and crisp. Remove bacon and onion from skillet using a slotted spoon; drain on paper towels. Reserve bacon drippings in the skillet.

Add brown sugar to drippings and cook over low heat until mixture thickens, stirring constantly. Add vinegar and simmer until sugar is dissolved, stirring often. Stir in flour and enough water to make a thick sauce. Simmer for 15 minutes, stirring frequently. Add salt and mix well.

Pour mixture over potatoes and sprinkle top with reserved bacon and onion. Serve warm or at room temperature.

Yield: 8 to 10 servings

OVEN-ROASTED BARBEQUED BRISKET

1 (6-pound) beef brisket or
 shoulder roast

1 teaspoon seasoned salt

½ teaspoon celery salt

½ teaspoon garlic salt

½ teaspoon onion salt

Pepper to taste

½ cup liquid smoke

2 tablespoons Worcestershire sauce

1 cup Barbeque Sauce (page 133)

Coat brisket with seasoned salts, pepper and liquid smoke. Cover with foil and then refrigerate.

Preheat oven to 250 degrees. Remove brisket from refrigerator and discard foil. Sprinkle brisket with Worcestershire sauce. Wrap tightly in foil and place on a large baking pan.

Bake for five hours. Uncover and baste generously with Barbeque Sauce. Bake for one hour longer. Cool slightly and then refrigerate. Skim off and discard the fat. Slice and serve warm or at room temperature.

Serve with Barbeque Sauce and Sauerkraut Slaw (page 133) on Sister Schubert's Dinner Yeast Rolls for tasty sliders.

BARBEQUE SAUCE

1	medium onion, chopped
3	tablespoons ketchup
2	tablespoons white vinegar
1	tablespoon lemon juice
2	tablespoons Worcestershire sauce
¼	cup water
1	teaspoon paprika
3	tablespoons brown sugar
1	teaspoon salt
1	teaspoon chili powder
½	teaspoon ground red pepper
1	teaspoon dry mustard
½	cup unsalted butter

Mix all ingredients in a saucepan and simmer for 5 minutes. Use as a sauce for chicken, pork, beef or lamb.

Yield: 1 cup

SAUERKRAUT SLAW FOR SLIDERS

1¾	cups sugar
1	cup white vinegar
1	cup chopped onion
1	cup chopped celery
1	cup chopped green bell pepper
1	cup chopped red bell pepper

1	cup drained and chopped stuffed olives
1	(29-ounce) can sauerkraut, drained and rinsed
1	(14-ounce) can bean sprouts, optional

Combine sugar and vinegar in a medium saucepan. Bring to a boil; remove from heat and let stand to cool. Mix onion, celery, bell peppers, olives, sauerkraut and bean sprouts in a large glass bowl. Pour cooled vinegar mixture over vegetables, tossing to coat. Chill before serving.

Yield: 10 to 12 servings

GREG'S BARBEQUED BABY BACK PORK RIBS

8 pounds baby back pork ribs

Barbeque Sauce

Add ribs to a large stockpot. Pour in cold water to cover ribs and bring to a boil. Boil for 15 minutes and drain.

Preheat oven to 300 degrees. Line a roasting pan with foil and set aside.

Using paper towels, pat ribs dry on both sides. Arrange ribs on prepared pan and cover tightly with foil. Bake for two hours or until cooked through and tender. Cut into serving pieces.

Prepare the grill and grill ribs over hot coals for 15 to 20 minutes, turning and basting with Barbeque Sauce. Serve with additional sauce at room temperature.

....

Barbeque Sauce

2 tablespoons unsalted butter

1 small onion, finely chopped

1 clove garlic, finely chopped

3 tablespoons lemon juice

1 tablespoon soy sauce

1 tablespoon Worcestershire sauce

2 teaspoons hot red pepper sauce

3 cups ketchup

½ cup firmly packed brown sugar

½ cup water

Combine all ingredients in a medium saucepan. Bring mixture to a boil, stirring constantly. Reduce the heat. Simmer until flavors are blended and sauce reaches the desired consistency, stirring frequently. Cool, place in jar with lid and store in refrigerator for up to 2 weeks.

I think that people who are not interested in food always seem dry and unloving and don't have a real gusto for life.

JULIA CHILD

STRAWBERRY SHORTCAKES

1   pint blueberries

1   pint strawberries

Sister's Tea Cakes

Sweetened Vanilla Cream

Small fresh mint leaves for garnish

Wash and dry blueberries. Wash, dry and hull strawberries. Slice strawberries into ¼-inch slices.

To assemble shortcakes, place a single layer of Sister's Tea Cakes on a large serving platter. Add a layer of strawberries and a few blueberries

to the top of each tea cake. Top each with another tea cake and another layer of strawberries; add a dollop of Sweetened Vanilla Cream. Sprinkle with blueberries and add a few small mint leaves for garnish.

Yield: 3 dozen

SISTER'S TEA CAKES

3   cups all-purpose flour

¾   cup confectioners' sugar

1½   teaspoons salt

1   cup shortening

8   tablespoons cold water

Mix flour, sugar and salt in a large mixing bowl. Cut in shortening with two knives or a pastry blender until shortening is about the size of small peas.

Add cold water, a little at a time, until dough is sticky and holds together well. Divide dough in half and flatten each half into a disc. Wrap each in plastic wrap and chill in refrigerator for 30 minutes.

Preheat oven to 375 degrees. Line baking sheets with parchment and set aside.

Roll dough out on a lightly floured surface to a thickness of about ⅛ to ¼ inch. Cut dough out with 2- or 3-inch biscuit cutters. Place on prepared pans and bake until lightly browned, about 10 to 12 minutes.

Yield: 6 dozen

SWEETENED VANILLA CREAM

1   cup heavy cream

3   tablespoons sugar

1   teaspoon vanilla

In a chilled bowl, whip cream to soft peaks. Gradually beat in sugar and vanilla until the cream reaches a slightly stiffer stage.

CHRISSIE'S SUGAR COOKIES

3½	sticks unsalted butter, softened
3½	cups sugar
5	large eggs
8	cups all-purpose flour
1½	tablespoons baking powder
4	teaspoons vanilla extract
4	teaspoons almond extract

Cream butter and sugar on medium speed of mixer until creamy. Add eggs, one at a time, until combined. Sift flour and baking powder together. Add flour one cup at a time until well combined. Add vanilla and almond extracts.

Divide dough into two balls, wrap each in plastic wrap and refrigerate for one hour.

Preheat oven to 350 degrees. Lightly grease a baking sheet and set aside.

On a lightly floured surface, roll dough to ¼-inch thickness. Using assorted flag, star and patriotic cutters, cut cookies and place two inches apart on prepared baking sheet. Repeat with remaining dough.

Bake cookies for 10 to 12 minutes or until edges are lightly browned. Cool on baking sheet for two minutes and remove to wire rack to cool completely.

Yield: About 60 cookies, depending on cookie cutter size

HOW TO DECORATE COOKIES LIKE CHRISSIE!

Your local crafts store will have the basic supplies you will need to get started, including professional paste colors, 10-inch disposable icing bags and decorating tips. You will need a different bag and decorating tip for each color frosting you plan to use.

For most simple designs, small to medium round tips and small to medium star tips will work best.

Once your icings are prepared, cover the surface of each one with damp paper towels to prevent their drying out.

Place cooled cookies on wax paper and outline the design and top edge of each cookie with icing using a small round tip. Allow outlines to dry completely.

Using a larger round tip, carefully flow icing into prepared outline. You may need to thin the flow icing slightly by adding water a drop or two at a time until it reaches workable consistency.

Allow base icing to dry completely before piping monograms, stars or other surface decorations. Start simple but give it a try…you can do it!

CHRISSIE'S DECORATING ICING

3   tablespoons meringue powder

1   (16-ounce) box confectioners' sugar

6 to 8   tablespoons water

Professional paste colors

Combine all ingredients except paste color in mixer bowl and mix until smooth. Divide icing into portions for as many colors as you plan to use; add paste color to each to achieve desired colors.

Spoon icing into bags with appropriate tips. Remember to keep icing covered that is not immediately being used.

BIRTHDAY BASH

Cinco de Mayo Style

I If you are lucky enough to have been born on the Mexican holiday, Cinco de Mayo, your birthday party will be a double celebration! This party tradition began when Sister's son, Evans, was born, and always provides a colorful theme for his birthday celebration.

Mexico's red, white, and green flag are the colors of the day, and no South of the Border theme is complete without a piñata filled with candy. A delightful Taco Bar with all the fixings is the centerpiece of the spread that features spicy and sweet accompaniment to the overall spirit of fiesta. Feliz Cumpleaños!

MENU

Soft Drinks

Lemonade

Homemade Guacamole

Chile con Queso

Taco Bar

Pralines

Chocolate Pound Cake

HOMEMADE GUACAMOLE

6   very ripe avocados

2   green onions, finely chopped (green and white parts)

2   medium tomatoes, chopped

2   garlic cloves, minced

1   tablespoon minced fresh cilantro

1   teaspoon Worcestershire sauce

Tabasco sauce to taste

2   teaspoons salt

Juice of 2 limes or lemons

Peel and dice avocados, saving the pits. Add onions, tomatoes, garlic, cilantro and seasonings; stir in lime juice. Mash with a potato masher to blend, leaving some of the avocado in larger pieces for texture. Spoon mixture into a serving bowl.

If making guacamole ahead of time, take preventative measures to keep it from turning dark. Return the avocado pits to the bowl and sprinkle the top with additional lime or lemon juice. Cover with plastic wrap, pressing it as close to the surface of the dip as possible. The goal is to prevent as much air as possible from coming into contact with the dip. Remove pits and stir gently when ready to serve.

Yield: 4 cups

 Here is a quick and easy way to prepare avocados. Using a small, sharp knife, slice avocados lengthwise to the pit. Gently twist the sides in opposite directions and pull apart. Remove pit by "hacking" into it with a knife and lifting it out. Then if you want the flesh diced, cut it in both directions while still in the skin and scoop it out using a large tablespoon. If you plan to mash it or use the flesh for other purposes, simply scoop it out while still in one piece.

CHILE CON QUESO

3   tablespoons olive oil

1   medium onion, peeled and chopped

1   (4-ounce) can pickled whole jalapeño peppers, drained and chopped

1   (13-ounce) can evaporated milk

1   (2-pound) package processed cheese product, cubed

1   teaspoon Tabasco

Heat olive oil in a skillet and sauté onion. Stir in jalapeños and set aside.

In the top of a double boiler, over simmering water, place evaporated milk, cheese cubes and Tabasco. Stir until cheese is thoroughly melted. Add reserved onion mixture and blend well.

Serve in a chafing dish along with tostados or tortilla chips.

Yield: 1 quart

 To make a milder version of this dip, adjust the number of jalapeños and the amount of Tabasco you use. If you have bacon drippings on hand, they may be used to sauté the onion to add flavor.

To make in microwave, place all ingredients in a 2-quart glass container and heat on half power, stirring frequently, until melted.

TACO BAR

Taco Meat

¼   cup olive oil

½   onion, chopped

2   garlic cloves, minced

1   pound lean ground beef

1   teaspoon salt

2   teaspoons chili powder

¼   cup chili sauce

½   teaspoon cumin

Heat oil in a large skillet over medium heat and sauté onion and garlic until translucent. Stir in crumbled beef, salt and chili powder. Sauté until beef is browned, breaking it up with the back of a wooden spoon while cooking. Stir in chili sauce and cumin. Spoon out as much excess oil as possible and keep meat mixture warm.

Yield: filling for 12 tacos

Hard Taco Shells

1   cup shortening for frying

12   small corn tortillas

Melt shortening in a large skillet over medium-high heat. Drop tortillas in oil, one or two at a time, and heat until they become limp. Remove from oil and carefully fold in half. Return to skillet and continue to fry until crisp. Drain on paper towels before serving.

NOTE: Offer your guest a choice of soft and hard taco shells. Small flour tortillas are easy to work with and make a delicioso taco!

NOTE: For a large crowd, purchasing ready-made taco shells will save both time and energy.

Taco Toppings

Chopped green onion

Grated sharp Cheddar cheese

Grated Monterey Jack cheese

Shredded iceberg lettuce

Diced tomatoes

Jalapeño peppers, seeded and chopped

Chunky salsa

Queso blanco

Sour cream

To prepare your Taco Bar, set up table in an area easily accessible by guests. Put taco shells in a lined basket at the head of the table, followed by a bowl or small chafing dish holding the meat filling.

Place topping ingredients in individual bowls and arrange along the table so that guests may select their favorite toppings and build their own taco.

PRALINES

2	cups light brown sugar, firmly packed
½	cup Pet evaporated milk
3	tablespoons unsalted butter
2	cups coarsely chopped pecans
1	teaspoon vanilla extract

Line a large baking sheet with wax paper and set aside.

Place sugar, milk and butter in a heavy-bottomed saucepan. Cook over medium heat, stirring constantly, to slightly under soft ball stage (236 degrees). Stir in pecans and vanilla.

Let cool to lukewarm while continuously beating the mixture. Drop mixture in mounds onto the prepared baking sheet. Allow pralines to rest until set.

Yield: 24 pralines

SISTER Says! If you aren't using a candy thermometer, test for "soft ball stage" by dropping a teaspoon of the mixture into a cup of cold water. If it makes a ball that will flatten on its own when removed from the water, then it is cooked correctly.

LEMONADE

3 cups sugar

12 cups water, divided

Juice of 20 lemons, about 3 cups

In a small heavy saucepan, add sugar and three cups water. Cook over low heat until mixture is clear and sugar is dissolved; increase heat and boil for about one minute. Remove from heat and cool slightly.

Add nine cups of water to a large pitcher or beverage jar. Stir in cooled syrup and lemon juice and blend well.

Yield: 1 gallon

 SISTER *Says!* To get the most juice out of fresh lemons, bring them to room temperature and roll them under your palm on the kitchen counter before squeezing.

CHOCOLATE POUND CAKE

1 cup unsalted butter, softened

½ cup solid shortening, softened

3 cups sugar

5 eggs

3 cups all-purpose flour

½ teaspoon baking powder

½ teaspoon salt

4 tablespoons cocoa

1 cup milk

1 tablespoon vanilla extract

Preheat oven to 325 degrees. Grease and flour a Bundt pan or tube pan and set aside.

Cream together butter, shortening and sugar until smooth. Add eggs, one at a time, beating well after each addition. Sift together flour, baking powder, salt and cocoa and add alternately with milk. Beat in vanilla. Pour mixture into prepared pan.

Bake for 1 hour and 20 minutes. Test for doneness. Allow cake to cool in pan for 15 minutes; invert onto a plate. Cool before icing.

Icing

½ cup unsalted butter

3 tablespoons cocoa

6 tablespoons milk

1 (1-pound) box confectioners' sugar, sifted

1 teaspoon vanilla extract

Add butter, cocoa and milk to a saucepan. Heat over low heat until butter is melted and mixture is bubbling. Remove from heat and add sugar and vanilla. Beat until smooth and frost cake.

Yield: 12 to 15 servings

NOTE: To make a delicious yellow pound cake, omit cocoa from cake recipe and prepare as otherwise directed.

Family Celebrations

SUNDAY
Dinner

Sunday dinner is one of our very favorite memories, at Mom's or Grandmother's house. Both of us grew up in small towns—Sister in Troy, Alabama, and Betty in Cartersville, Georgia. We found that our early lives were very similar. Each of us loved to cook, and learned from our mothers and grandmothers, and from the talented women who cooked for our families. We have treasured their instruction and worked hard to make memories for our own families from the recipes they taught us.

This Sunday Dinner menu begins with chicken. Fried Chicken is the standard, but when you are trying to get the family to Sunday School and church on time, Chicken and Dressing is a convenient and flavorful alternative.

We believe these recipes will bring a satisfied smile to every face at the table!

SWEET TEA

2   family-size tea bags

2   cups sugar

Sprigs of fresh mint

Lemon slices

Brew tea according to package directions. Pour into a one-gallon container. Add sugar to warm tea and stir to dissolve. Fill jar with cold water and stir again. Chill and serve over crushed ice. Garnish with mint sprigs and lemon slices.

Yield: 1 gallon

THE BEST FRIED CHICKEN AND GRAVY

2   (2- to 3-pound) broiler-fryer chickens, cut up

2   cups buttermilk

2   cups all-purpose flour

½   teaspoon salt

½   teaspoon black pepper

Canola oil for frying

Place chicken pieces in a large flat dish. Pour buttermilk over the pieces, cover with plastic wrap and refrigerate for at least one hour. Combine flour, salt and pepper in a large ziptop bag.

Drain the chicken pieces and toss them, one at a time, in the flour mixture. Shake off any excess flour and place the pieces on wax paper to dry.

Heat ⅛ to ¼ inch of oil in a large, heavy skillet. Fry chicken pieces until just browned on all sides. Cover and simmer, turning occasionally, for 40 to 45 minutes. Test to see that chicken is tender and that the juices all run clear when meat is pierced. Remove chicken from pan and keep warm while making Gravy.

Gravy

½   cup fried chicken drippings

6   tablespoons all-purpose flour

2   cups milk

3   cups water

Salt and pepper to taste

Drain all but ½ cup of drippings from skillet where chicken was cooked. Over medium heat, sprinkle flour into drippings and stir until bubbly and thick and slightly browned. Add milk and water and whisk to blend. Add more water if gravy appears too thick. Season with salt and pepper to desired taste.

Serve with the chicken and rice.

Yield: 12 servings

NOTE: If your family likes "white meat," three pounds of bone-in chicken breasts may be substituted for the cut-up fryers.

SLOW COOKER CHICKEN AND CORNBREAD DRESSING

1 rotisserie chicken, meat pulled from bone

Cornbread, crumbled

8 slices day-old bread, torn

2 stalks celery, chopped

1 yellow onion, chopped

2 garlic cloves, chopped

4 tablespoons chopped fresh sage

2 tablespoons chopped fresh thyme

1 teaspoon kosher salt

1 teaspoon ground black pepper

4 eggs, lightly beaten

2 (14-ounce) cans chicken broth

2 (10.75-ounce) cans cream of chicken soup

1 (10.75-ounce) can cream of mushroom soup

3 tablespoons butter

Place chicken, cornbread, bread, celery, onion, garlic, herbs, salt and pepper in a 4-quart or larger slow cooker. Stir to combine.

In a large bowl, whisk together eggs, chicken broth and soups. Pour into slow cooker. Stir to combine. Dot with butter. Cook on high for three hours or on low for four to five hours. Stir halfway through cooking time.

Yield: 10 to 12 servings

....

Cornbread

1 egg, lightly beaten

2 cups buttermilk

2 cups self-rising yellow cornmeal mix

¼ teaspoon salt

½ cup butter, melted

Preheat oven to 450 degrees. Lightly grease a 10-inch cast-iron skillet and place it in the oven to heat.

In a large bowl, combine egg and buttermilk, stirring well. Add cornmeal and salt, stirring until ingredients are combined. Add melted butter, stirring to combine. Pour mixture into hot skillet.

Bake 15 to 20 minutes or until cornbread is golden brown and begins to pull away from the sides of the skillet. Let cool in skillet for 20 minutes. Remove to a wire rack to cool completely.

Yield: 1 (10-inch) skillet of cornbread

Truffles taking it easy on Sunday

MAPLE-GLAZED BRUSSELS SPROUTS

4 tablespoons unsalted butter, divided

2 pounds Brussels sprouts, trimmed and halved

½ cup chicken broth

2 tablespoons maple syrup, divided

1 teaspoon minced fresh thyme

1 tablespoon cider vinegar

Salt and pepper

Melt two tablespoons butter in a 12-inch skillet over medium-high heat. Add Brussels sprouts and cook until browned, about six to eight minutes. Stir in broth, 1 tablespoon maple syrup and thyme and cook over medium-low heat, covered, until Brussels sprouts are nearly tender, an additional six to eight minutes.

Uncover and increase heat to medium-high. Cook until liquid is nearly evaporated, about five minutes. Remove from heat and stir in vinegar, remaining butter and remaining maple syrup. Season to taste with salt and pepper before serving.

Yield: 8 to 10 servings

BETTY'S *Best!* If you usually purchase frozen Brussels sprouts and need some help getting the right fresh ones, here is a tip. Choose small, tight heads that are no more than 1½ inches in diameter. They will be tender and perfect for this preparation.

CHEDDAR DROP BISCUITS

2½ cups all-purpose flour (we prefer White Lily flour for our biscuits)

2 tablespoons sugar

1 tablespoon baking powder

1 teaspoon kosher salt

6 tablespoons cold unsalted butter, cubed

1 cup shredded sharp Cheddar cheese

1 cup buttermilk

1 egg, lightly beaten

Preheat oven to 450 degrees. Lightly grease a baking sheet and set aside.

Add flour, sugar, baking powder and salt to the bowl of a food processor. Process until well mixed. Add cold butter gradually and process until the consistency of cornmeal. Empty mixture into a medium mixing bowl. Add cheese and mix well.

In a small bowl, combine buttermilk and egg; mix well. Add to flour mixture and stir until just moistened; it should not be smooth. Drop batter by large tablespoons on the prepared baking sheet. Bake 15 minutes or until tops are golden brown. Serve immediately.

Yield: 12 medium biscuits

SISTER *Says!* In the Deep South, the midday meal is often referred to as dinner, and the evening meal is supper.

RAINBOW COLE SLAW

RAINBOW COLE SLAW

2 cups shredded green cabbage

2 cups shredded red cabbage

1 carrot, grated

⅓ cup finely chopped onion, optional

¼ cup chopped red bell pepper

1 tablespoon chopped fresh parsley

½ cup sour cream

¾ cup mayonnaise

2 teaspoons sugar

1 teaspoon cider vinegar

Salt and pepper to taste

Combine all vegetables and parsley in a large mixing bowl. In a separate bowl, stir together sour cream, mayonnaise, sugar and vinegar. Blend well and pour over vegetables; mix gently. Salt and pepper to taste.

Cover and refrigerate until chilled.

Yield: 12 or more servings

NALL'S OLD-FASHIONED BANANA PUDDING

Microwave Custard

1 cup sugar

1 teaspoon salt

¼ cup cornstarch

5 cups whole milk

8 egg yolks, beaten

4 teaspoons vanilla extract

Mix sugar, salt and cornstarch in a 2-quart glass bowl or measuring cup. Stir in milk gradually. Microwave on high for seven minutes or until slightly thickened, whisking every three minutes. In a separate bowl, stir slightly more than half the custard into the egg yolks.

Whisk yolk mixture into remaining custard in glass cup. Add vanilla and whisk until well combined.

Pudding Assembly

1 box vanilla wafer cookies

4 ripe bananas, sliced

In a large ovenproof serving bowl, alternate layers of vanilla wafers, bananas and prepared custard. Top with meringue.

Meringue

4 egg whites

½ teaspoon cream of tartar

6 tablespoons sugar

1 teaspoon vanilla

Preheat oven to 350 degrees. Whip egg whites with cream of tartar until stiff, but not dry. They should stand in peaks but tip slightly when beaters are removed.

Beat in sugar, one tablespoon at a time. Beat in vanilla and spoon mixture over top of prepared pudding. Bake for 10 to 15 minutes or until meringue is light brown.

Yield: 6 to 8 servings

DOUBLE PEACH PIE

Filling

1 ½ quarts peaches, peeled and chopped

1 ½ cups sugar

½ cup unsalted butter, melted

1 teaspoon cinnamon

½ teaspoon nutmeg

¼ teaspoon salt

1 cup water

In a large mixing bowl, stir all filling ingredients together. Divide mixture in half and set aside.

Pastry

3 cups all-purpose flour

1 teaspoon salt

1 cup shortening

6 to 8 tablespoons cold water

Cinnamon sugar to taste

Mix flour and salt in a large mixing bowl. Cut in shortening with a fork or pastry blender. Add cold water, a little at a time, until dough is sticky and holds together well. Shape pastry into a ball; wrap in plastic wrap and chill for 30 minutes.

Preheat oven to 375 degrees.

Divide pastry dough in half and roll each into a thin rectangle that will fit a 9×13×2-inch baking dish. Spoon half the filling into the baking dish and cover with one piece of the pastry; pierce randomly with a fork.

Bake until crust is just golden brown and filling is bubbly, about 30 minutes. Remove from oven and carefully press crust down into the filling.

Spoon remaining half of filling over the baked crust and cover with remaining pastry sheet. Pierce with a fork, sprinkle with cinnamon sugar and bake 25 to 30 minutes or until top crust is golden brown.

Serve warm with a scoop of vanilla bean ice cream.

Yield: 10 to 12 servings

NOTE: A woven lattice crust makes a homemade pie look so pretty. While it might seem difficult, it is really quite easy. Prepare the pie as noted up to adding the top pastry. If the dough has softened too much, it will be more difficult to work with and you may need to chill it in the freezer for a few minutes. With the dough rolled out to the size of your pie, cut the dough into even strips, 1/2 to 3/4 inch wide. A pizza cuter works well for cutting. Lay out parallel strips of dough 1/2 inch apart on top of the filling. One at a time, beginning in the center, take remaining strips and place perpendicular, weaving over and under the parallel strips. As you work toward the outer edges, you will need to cut the length of the strips as needed.

Tailgating

A HOUSE DIVIDED

Food may be the ONLY thing people agree on when tailgating!
Our houses are truly divided as George and Sister are life-long Auburn fans and Betty and Bill wear Tennessee orange every fall weekend. So it's a good thing when food can soothe the evil beast that is Southeastern Conference Football.

To save our energy for cheering, we prefer dishes that can be prepared ahead of time and will travel well. And, since football fans are usually on their feet, the food needs to be portable and easy to eat. Pack colorful disposable plates and utensils, napkins, and cheer gear. Add your favorite libations and don't forget a thermos of tea or lemonade for the designated driver.

This menu checks off everything required. The dips are easy to make and refrigerate until departure. Your tailgate table features make ahead dips, filled rolls, sandwiches, a beautiful layered salad, dessert bars, and sugar cookies decorated in your school colors—just in case anyone needs a reminder of which side you're rooting for!

MENU

Cucumber Dip

Dirty Corn Dip

Ham Delights

Southern Pimiento Cheese
Sliders

Chicken Drumettes

Seven-Layer Salad

Sister's Sugar Cookies with
Chrissie's Decorations

Derby Day Bars

DIRTY CORN DIP

1	can diced tomatoes with chilies, drained
16	ounces whipped cream cheese
1	cup chipotle salsa
¾	cup mayonnaise
2	cups finely shredded Cheddar cheese
2	cans white niblet corn, drained

Combine all ingredients in a large bowl and stir well to blend. Refrigerate for several hours before serving. Serve with corn chips.

Yield: 30 servings

CUCUMBER DIP

2 (8-ounce) packages cream cheese, softened

1 (16-ounce) container sour cream

3 English cucumbers, grated and squeezed dry

½ cup chopped fresh dill

1 tablespoon fresh lemon juice

1 teaspoon seasoned salt

1 teaspoon hot sauce

1 teaspoon garlic powder

Fresh dill sprigs for garnish

In a medium bowl, beat cream cheese at medium speed with an electric mixer until smooth and creamy. Add sour cream, cucumber, dill, lemon juice, seasoned salt, hot sauce and garlic powder, beating to combine well.

Cover and refrigerate until ready to serve. Garnish with fresh dill sprigs if desired.

Serve with lavosh or your favorite snack crackers.

Yield: 25 appetizer servings

HAM DELIGHTS

½ cup unsalted butter, softened

2 tablespoons prepared mustard

½ teaspoon Worcestershire sauce

1 tablespoon poppy seeds

3 green onions, chopped

1 pound honey ham, shaved and chopped

6 ounces grated Swiss cheese

4 ounces grated Parmesan

6 ounces grated sharp Cheddar cheese

2 pans Sister Schubert's® Parker House Style Rolls

Combine butter, mustard, Worcestershire, poppy seeds and green onions; stir until well mixed. Add ham and cheeses and mix well.

Preheat oven to 375 degrees.

Remove rolls from pan and place one teaspoon filling inside each roll. Return filled rolls to pan and cover with foil. Bake for 15 to 20 minutes or until warm. Rolls may be filled ahead of time and covered and refrigerated until time to heat and serve.

Yield: 2 to 3 dozen rolls

CHICKEN DRUMETTES

12 to 15 chicken drumettes
    (3 to 3 ½ pounds)

Sea salt

1   cup all-purpose flour

3   teaspoons paprika

3   teaspoons black pepper

2 to 2½ cups solid shortening

Wash chicken in cold water and shake off excess moisture (do not dry or the flour mixture will not adhere). Sprinkle chicken with sea salt.

Combine flour, paprika and pepper in a large, heavy-duty ziptop bag, shaking to mix ingredients. Add five or six drumette pieces at a time and shake vigorously until thoroughly coated.

Heat shortening (1 ¼ inches deep) in a 12-inch cast-iron skillet to 360 to 365 degrees or until a drop of water sizzles when carefully added to the skillet. Add drumettes until skillet is full, but not crowded. Fry chicken one side at a time, nudging the drumettes so they don't stick to skillet, and turn gently with tongs.

Fry chicken until a light golden brown, 8 to 10 minutes. If the chicken is especially meaty, they may require a minute or so longer; just be careful not to fry so long that they dry out. Rest assured, these drumettes are just as good at room temperature as they are hot and will be a favorite at your tailgates.

Serve with Barbeque Dipping Sauce.

Yield: 6 appetizer servings

SISTER Says! You can't get more Southern than any kind of fried chicken! If you do not have a well-seasoned cast-iron frying pan, do not despair. Use any large, heavy skillet with a lid, or even an electric skillet.

Here are my secrets for perfect fried chicken: Use solid shortening and not cooking oil. Make sure the shortening is hot enough and keep an eye on the temperature throughout cooking. Never use a fork to turn fried chicken; if you puncture the skin, the juices will run out and your chicken will be dry. You can fry these delicious drumettes…just try!

BARBEQUE DIPPING SAUCE

½   cup apple cider vinegar

1   cup ketchup

2   tablespoons Worcestershire

2   tablespoons sugar

1   teaspoon salt

1   teaspoon dry mustard

Add vinegar, ketchup and Worcestershire to a small heavy saucepan and whisk to blend. Stir in dry ingredients and mix well.

Bring mixture to boiling over medium-high heat, stirring often. Use immediately or store in a covered jar and refrigerate for later use. Sauce keeps well.

SOUTHERN PIMIENTO CHEESE SLIDERS

2 pounds lean ground beef

1 teaspoon salt

1 teaspoon ground black pepper

Green leaf lettuce

1 package Sister Schubert's®
   Dinner Yeast Rolls, split

1½ cups Noel's Special Pimiento
    Cheese (page 115)

Heat a grill pan over medium-high heat. In a large bowl, gently combine beef, salt and pepper. Shape mixture into 12 small patties. Grill in pan for five minutes per side or until desired degree of doneness.

Place a small piece of lettuce and patties on bottom half of rolls. Spread two tablespoons pimiento cheese over each patty and top with roll tops.

Yield: 12 sliders

SEVEN-LAYER SALAD

5   cups chopped green leaf lettuce

2   cups seeded, chopped tomatoes

2   cups chopped yellow bell pepper

1   (12-ounce) package frozen green peas, thawed

2   cups chopped radish

2   cups diced seedless cucumber

Seven-Layer Salad Dressing

Shredded Cheddar cheese for garnish

Cooked crumbled bacon for garnish

In a 3 ½-quart glass bowl, layer lettuce, tomatoes, pepper, peas, radish and cucumber. Pour dressing over the top and smooth to edges of the bowl to seal. Cover tightly with plastic wrap and refrigerate at least four hours or as long as overnight. When ready to serve, sprinkle top of salad with cheese and bacon.

Yield: 8 to 10 servings

....

Seven-Layer Salad Dressing

2   cups mayonnaise

¼   cup chopped fresh chives

¼   cup chopped fresh dill

4   teaspoons Dijon mustard

2   teaspoons onion powder

½   teaspoon ground black pepper

In a small bowl, combine mayonnaise, chives, dill, Dijon, onion powder and pepper, stirring well.

Yield: 2 cups dressing

No man can be wise on an empty stomach.

ANONYMOUS

SISTER'S SUGAR COOKIES WITH CHRISSIE'S DECORATIONS

¾   **cup unsalted butter, softened**

1 ¼   **cups granulated sugar**

1   **egg**

½   **teaspoon vanilla**

½   **teaspoon almond extract**

2   **cups all-purpose flour**

½   **teaspoon salt**

¼   **teaspoon baking powder**

In a large mixing bowl, cream together butter and sugar. Beat in egg, vanilla and almond extract. In another bowl, stir together flour, salt and baking powder. Stir into creamed mixture and blend.

Preheat oven to 375 degrees. Divide dough in half and wrap each in plastic wrap. Chill pastry for 30 minutes. Roll each ball of dough into a ¼-inch thickness. Cut out with cookie cutters of desired shapes. Place cookies on baking sheets and bake for 10 to 12 minutes.

Yield: About 30 cookies, depending on cookie cutter size

SEE CHRISSIE'S ICING AND DECORATING TIPS ON PAGE 137.

DERBY DAY BARS

Crust

3	cups graham cracker crumbs
½	cup unsalted butter, melted
⅓	cup sugar
1	large egg white, lightly beaten

Filling

1	cup firmly packed light brown sugar
½	cup light corn syrup
½	cup dark corn syrup
¼	cup butter, melted
3	large eggs, lightly beaten
2	teaspoons vanilla extract
¼	teaspoon salt
2	cups chopped pecans
1	(12-ounce) package miniature semisweet chocolate chips

Preheat oven to 350 degrees. Line a 13×9-inch baking pan with heavy-duty foil. Spray foil with nonstick baking spray with flour and set aside.

For crust, in a medium bowl, combine graham cracker crumbs, melted butter, sugar and egg white, stirring until well combined. Press mixture into bottom of prepared pan. Bake for 10 minutes and cool completely.

For filling, in a large bowl, combine brown sugar and corn syrups. Add melted butter, eggs, vanilla and salt, whisking until well combined. Stir in pecans and chocolate chips; spoon mixture over prepared crust. Bake for 35 to 40 minutes or until middle is set.

Yield: 2 dozen bars

MAMA'S WHIPPED CREAM POUND CAKE

1	cup unsalted butter, softened
3	cups sugar, sifted
3	cups cake flour, sifted
8	large eggs, room temperature
1	teaspoon vanilla extract
1	teaspoon almond extract
2	teaspoons brandy
1	cup heavy cream

Grease and flour a 10-inch tube pan or 10-inch Bundt pan.

Using large bowl of mixer on high speed, cream butter until fluffy, about 10 minutes. Add sugar gradually, two tablespoons at a time, beating well after each addition.

Add ½ cup flour at a time and eggs one at a time alternately, beginning and ending with flour. Batter should be very smooth. Combine extracts and brandy with cream. Add cream mixture gradually, beating until well combined.

Pour batter into prepared pan, being careful not to spill batter on sides. Place pan on center rack in cold oven. Turn heat to 325 degrees and bake for 1 hour and 25 minutes. Do not open oven door while baking.

Remove cake to a wire rack and cool in the pan for 15 minutes. Turn out onto rack to cool completely.

Yield: 1 large cake

SISTER Says! This family recipe dates back to the early 1900s and is truly spectacular. Follow the instructions as given, even though the method seems strange to modern bakers. You must not open the oven door to check on your cake. If you must look, turn on the oven light for a quick peek through the glass.

Did you know that when you turn on that light, a small new heat source begins, which can skew the shape of your cake? If you do look, remember to turn off the light immediately afterward.

Mama says not to fret if there is a small moist "sad streak" in the center; that's her favorite part.

**MAMA'S WHIPPED
CREAM POUND CAKE**

DERBY DAY BARS

Celebrations for Every Day

POOL PARTY
At Sister's
HOUSE

Summer comes early to Alabama, and well before June, Sister plans the first pool party of the season, because the water is never too cold for the grandchildren! The cabana kitchen is designed for outdoor entertaining, making preparations simple and convenient, and ample refrigerated storage keeps everything fresh and cold. Serving trays, barware, and dishes are plastic, to ensure safety around the pool, and add a colorful accent to every dish. Stacks of bright beach towels and cheerful pots of multicolored flowers make an inviting setting for a day at the pool.

MENU

Blended Mojitos

Creamy Mango Mold

Shrimp with Red Sauce and
White Rémoulade

Marcona almonds and
toasted pecans

Watermelon Salad

Potato Swiss Salad

Corn Salad

Parmesan Chicken

Assorted Fruit with
Cinnamon Dip
and assorted cheeses

Cream Cheese Brownies

Lemon Tassies

BLENDED MOJITOS

We love these—blended Margarita-style and served in long, cooled glasses with a sugared rim.
A refreshing drink of lime, mint, and rum is the perfect cocktail for a summer evening.

12	fresh mint sprigs, each about 8 inches long
½	cup sugar
½	cup fresh lime juice
1	cup light rum
Sugar and lime wedges for coating rims	
Ice cubes	
2	cups club soda
½	cup loosely packed fresh mint leaves
1	lime, cut into 4 wedges for garnish
4	small fresh mint sprigs for garnish

In a medium bowl, using the back of a wooden spoon, crush together the mint sprigs, sugar and lime juice. Pour in rum, cover with plastic wrap and let stand at room temperature for at least two hours or as long as overnight.

Select four tall, slender glasses. Spread a layer of sugar on a small, flat plate. Working with one glass at a time, run a lime wedge around the edge of the glass to moisten it, and then dip the rim into the sugar to coat it evenly. Place glasses in the freezer to chill for at least 15 minutes.

When ready to make mojitos, fill a blender half full with ice cubes. Pour the rum mixture through a fine mesh sieve into the blender. Add club soda and the ½ cup of mint leaves and purée until well blended.

Divide the mixture evenly among the chilled glasses. Garnish each glass with a lime wedge and a mint sprig.

Yield: 4 servings

CREAMY MANGO MOLD

3	(3-ounce) packages lemon-flavored gelatin
1½	cups hot water
1	(29-ounce) can mangos in syrup, undrained
Juice of 1 lemon	
6	ounces cream cheese, softened
½	cup chopped peanuts
½	cup shredded sweetened coconut

Dissolve gelatin in hot water and set aside.

In the bowl of a food processor, add mangos with juice, lemon juice and cream cheese. Pulse until puréed. Add to cooled gelatin and blend well.

Pour into a lightly oiled decorative mold and chill until firmly set, about 5 hours or overnight.

Unmold onto a serving plate and garnish with peanuts and coconut.

Yield: 12 to 15 servings

SHRIMP WITH RED SAUCE AND WHITE RÉMOULADE

Shrimp

1   pound of large shrimp, steamed or boiled

Red Sauce

2   cups cocktail sauce

½   cup fresh horseradish (not prepared kind)

1   tablespoon lemon zest

½   teaspoon salt

Combine all ingredients and mix thoroughly. To store, spoon sauce into a glass jar with a tight-fitting lid and refrigerate for up to 4 days.

Yield: 2 ½ cups

White Rémoulade

1   cup premium mayonnaise

⅓   cup Creole mustard

3   entire green onions, finely chopped

1   tablespoon fresh lemon juice

2   tablespoons tarragon wine vinegar

2   tablespoons fresh parsley, finely chopped

½   teaspoon paprika

3   garlic cloves, minced

½   teaspoon cayenne pepper

1   tablespoon fresh tarragon, finely chopped (or ½ teaspoon dried)

Salt to taste

Combine all ingredients and mix thoroughly. To store, spoon sauce into a glass jar with a tight-fitting lid and refrigerate. Can be made 3 days ahead of time and is easily doubled. This is quite likely our favorite condiment for shrimp!

Yield: 1 ½ cups

 SISTER Says! Follow George's suggestions for perfect boiled shrimp on page 100.

WATERMELON SALAD

1 ½   cups watermelon cubes

¼   cup crumbled feta

Mint leaves, thinly sliced

Dark Balsamic Glaze

Salt and pepper to taste

In a medium salad bowl, toss together watermelon cubes, feta and mint leaves. Drizzle balsamic glaze over the top and salt and pepper to taste.

Yield: 4 servings

NOTE: Balsamic glaze can be found in supermarkets with the vinegars.

When one has tasted watermelons, one knows what angels eat.

MARK TWAIN

Assorted cheese tray; wheel of Brie, block of extra-sharp cheddar, block of baby Swiss and wedge of blue cheese.

ASSORTED FRUIT WITH CINNAMON DIP

1   cup sour cream

¼   cup firmly packed brown sugar

¼   teaspoon cinnamon

1   pound seedless red grapes, separated into small clusters

1   pound seedless green grapes, separated into small clusters

1   pint fresh blueberries

1   pint fresh raspberries

1   pint dark sweet cherries

1   cantaloupe, peeled and sliced

Combine sour cream, brown sugar and cinnamon in a small bowl and mix well.

Arrange grapes, blueberries, raspberries, cherries and cantaloupe on a serving platter; serve with Cinnamon Dip.

Yield: 8 to 10 servings

CORN SALAD

2 (16-ounce) packages frozen shoe peg corn, cooked and drained

1 green bell pepper, seeded and chopped

1 cup sliced cherry tomatoes, optional

½ cup chopped purple onion

¾ cup chopped cucumber

½ cup mayonnaise

¼ cup sour cream

1 tablespoon apple cider vinegar

½ teaspoon celery salt

½ teaspoon white pepper

Salt to taste

Combine corn, bell pepper, tomatoes, onion and cucumber in a large bowl and toss to mix.

In a small bowl, combine mayonnaise, sour cream, vinegar, celery salt, white pepper and salt to taste and whisk to blend. Pour over the corn mixture and mix well.

Refrigerate, covered, for at least three hours before serving.

Yield: 10 to 12 servings

PARMESAN CHICKEN

2 to 4 tablespoons white wine

½ cup Dijon mustard

1 cup fresh bread crumbs or panko

1 cup grated Parmesan

3 pounds boneless chicken breasts

Preheat oven to 375 degrees. Lightly grease a baking sheet and set aside.

In a shallow bowl, add enough wine to Dijon mustard to make a dipping consistency, mixing well. Combine bread crumbs and Parmesan in a shallow dish and mix well. Dip each chicken piece in the mustard mixture and then roll in bread crumb mixture to coat. Arrange chicken pieces on prepared baking sheet.

Bake for 45 minutes or until cooked through. This dish is equally tasty served hot or at room temperature, making it the perfect choice for a picnic basket.

Yield: 6 to 8 servings

PARMESAN CHICKEN

POTATO SWISS SALAD

3	pounds unpeeled small red or Yukon gold potatoes
6	hard-cooked eggs, chopped
¼	cup finely chopped onion
2 ¼	cups mayonnaise
6	tablespoons milk
1	teaspoon salt
1	teaspoon ground black pepper
1	cup shredded sharp Cheddar cheese
1	cup shredded Swiss cheese

Boil potatoes in enough water to cover in a large saucepan, just until tender. Drain and cool; cut into quarters into a large mixing bowl. Add eggs and onion and toss to mix.

In a small bowl, combine mayonnaise, milk, salt and pepper and whisk to mix. Add to potato mixture and mix well. Add the cheeses and stir to blend.

Chill, covered, until serving time.

Yield: 10 to 12 servings

SISTER *Says!* There are a lot of potato salad recipes in this book because it is my husband George's favorite side. He has not met a potato salad he doesn't love. But this is one of his favorites.

LEMON TASSIES AND
CREAM CHEESE BROWNIES

LEMON TASSIES

These Tassies make an impressive presentation; your guests will never know just how easy they are. To add nature's artwork, top each tart with a Johnny Jump-up or other small edible flower.

Flaky Pie Crust, prepared (page 35)

Betty's Lemon Curd, prepared (page 208)

Fresh raspberries or sweetened whipped cream

Let pastry come to room temperature. Preheat oven to 375 degrees. Spray mini muffin pan with cooking spray.

On a lightly floured surface, roll out pastry evenly, to ⅛ to ¼-inch thickness. Cut pastry with 1½-inch fluted cookie cutter. Place each round in muffin pan. Prick pastry with a fork and bake until lightly browned, 10 to 15 minutes.

Fill pastries with Betty's Lemon Curd and top with a fresh raspberry or a tiny dollop of sweetened whipped cream.

SISTER *Says!* Pastry shells can be made up to two weeks in advance. Store in an airtight container in a cool, dry place. Can also be frozen.

CREAM CHEESE BROWNIES

Brownies

1	cup unsifted all-purpose flour
1	teaspoon baking powder
½	teaspoon salt
1	cup coarsely chopped walnuts
8	ounces semisweet chocolate
6	tablespoons unsalted butter
4	eggs, lightly beaten
1½	cups sugar
½	teaspoon almond extract
2	teaspoons vanilla extract

Cream Cheese Topping

6	ounces cream cheese, softened
3	tablespoons butter, softened
½	cup sugar
2	eggs
2	tablespoons all-purpose flour
1	teaspoon vanilla extract

For brownie batter, mix flour, baking powder, salt and walnuts together. Melt chocolate and butter in a glass measuring cup in the microwave. Cool slightly. Beat the eggs in a medium mixing bowl; add sugar gradually, beating until well mixed. Stir in chocolate mixture and mix well. Add flour mixture and blend well. Stir in almond and vanilla extracts.

Preheat oven to 350 degrees. Butter and line a 9×12-inch baking pan with parchment and set aside.

For the cream cheese topping, beat the cream cheese and butter in a mixing bowl until smooth. Add sugar, eggs, flour and vanilla and mix well. Pour two-thirds of the chocolate batter into the baking pan. Spread with cream cheese topping. Spoon remaining chocolate batter over the cream cheese layer. Swirl with a knife to marble. Bake for 30 minutes or until a wooden toothpick inserted near the center comes out clean; do not over bake.

These are almost soufflé-like when they come out of the oven. Delicious warm or cold.

Cool in the pan before cutting to serve.

Yield: 12 servings

Celebrations for Every Day

Casual Supper
FOR FRIENDS

Wherever you live, we all like to believe that we have cornered the market on hospitality!

We have given many parties that needed advance planning and flawless execution, but some of our most memorable meals have been impromptu suppers for a few close friends. Not much preparation, and maybe a shortcut or two; easy and comforting, like friends we invite in through the kitchen door. Fire up the grill, chill some wine and beer, and make time to break bread with the special friends in your life.

MENU

Vidalia Onion Baked Dip

Pecan Beet Salad

Grilled Flank Steak with
Molasses Barbeque Glaze

or

Maple-Bourbon Glazed Salmon

Asiago Corn Pudding

Collard Greens with
Black-Eyed Peas

Sister's Broccoli Cornbread

Free-Form French Apple Tart

WINE SUGGESTION:

Côtes du Rhône Rouge

VIDALIA ONION BAKED DIP

2	tablespoons unsalted butter
3	large Vidalia onions, coarsely chopped
2	cups shredded Swiss cheese
2	cups mayonnaise
½	teaspoon Tabasco sauce
1	garlic clove, minced
1	(8-ounce) can sliced water chestnuts, drained
¼	cup white wine

Preheat oven to 375 degrees. Butter a 1 ½-quart casserole dish and set aside.

Melt butter in a large skillet and sauté onions until tender. In a large mixing bowl, combine cheese, mayonnaise, Tabasco, garlic, water chestnuts and wine. Stir to mix and add sautéed onions. Mix until well blended and spoon into prepared dish. Bake for 25 minutes.

Serve warm with tortilla chips or pita chips.

Yield: 4 cups

PECAN BEET SALAD

6 medium-sized golden or red beets
   (about 6 ounces each)

1 cup pecan halves

¼ cup rice wine vinegar

1 large shallot, minced

2 tablespoons light brown sugar

½ teaspoon salt

½ teaspoon freshly ground black
   pepper

½ teaspoon vanilla extract

¼ cup canola oil

1 (5-ounce) package gourmet
   mixed salad greens, washed

1 cup crumbled Gorgonzola cheese

Preheat oven to 325 degrees. Trim beet stems to one inch; gently wash beets. Wrap each one in a sheet of foil and place on a rimmed baking pan. Bake for one hour or until tender. Transfer beets to a wire rack and cool, still wrapped in foil, for 30 minutes.

Decrease oven temperature to 350 degrees. Spread pecan halves in a single layer on a rimmed baking sheet and bake five to seven minutes or until lightly toasted and fragrant, watching closely. Cool completely on a wire rack, about 15 minutes.

Whisk together vinegar, shallot, sugar, salt, pepper and vanilla in a small bowl. Drizzle oil into mixture in a slow, steady stream, whisking constantly until smooth and oil is incorporated.

Peel beets and remove stem ends. Cut beets into ½-inch wedges and gently toss with ⅓ cup vinegar mixture. Arrange salad greens on a serving platter. Toss with beet mixture, Gorgonzola cheese and pecans; serve with remaining vinaigrette.

Yield: 4 to 6 servings

GRILLED FLANK STEAK WITH MOLASSES BARBEQUE GLAZE

½	cup molasses
¼	cup coarse-grained mustard
1	tablespoon olive oil
1	(1 ½-pound) flank steak

Whisk together molasses, mustard and olive oil in a small bowl.

Place steak in a shallow dish or large ziptop freezer bag. Pour molasses mixture over steak, reserving ¼ cup for basting. Cover or seal and refrigerate, turning occasionally, for two hours. Remove meat from marinade, discarding excess marinade. Remove from refrigerator an hour before grilling.

Prepare grill and heat to medium-high (350 to 400 degrees).

Place steak on grill and cook, with lid closed, six minutes on each side or until desired degree of doneness, brushing often with reserved ¼ cup marinade. Remove steak from grill and tent loosely with foil; allow meat to rest for 10 minutes. Slice steak diagonally, across the grain, into very thin strips.

Yield: 6 servings

BETTY'S Best! This is a very flavorful cut of meat but will become tough if overcooked. Monitor it closely during grilling time.

Those who bring sunshine into the life of others cannot keep it from themselves.

ANONYMOUS

MAPLE-BOURBON GLAZED SALMON

¾ cup pure maple syrup

⅓ cup orange juice

3 tablespoons bourbon

4 (4- to 5-ounce) skinless salmon fillets

Salt and pepper to taste

¼ cup coarsely chopped pecans or walnuts

Preheat broiler and lightly grease broiler pan.

For glaze, in a small saucepan, combine syrup, orange juice and bourbon. Cook, uncovered, over medium heat while preparing salmon.

Lightly sprinkle fillets with salt and pepper and place on prepared broiler pan. Broil, three to four inches away from heat source, for about five minutes. Remove two tablespoons of glaze and brush salmon; turn pieces over and brush second side. Broil five additional minutes or until salmon flakes easily when tested with a fork.

Stir pecans into remaining glaze. Heat on high for about five minutes or until glaze reaches the consistency of thick syrup. Spoon pecan syrup over fillets and serve immediately.

Yield: 4 servings

BETTY'S Best! This salmon may also be prepared on the grill. Spray grid with nonstick cooking spray before heating grill. When grill is hot, place fillets on the grill, skin side down. Cook four to five minutes, depending on thickness of the salmon. Brush sides with syrup as in directions for broiling.

Jacob Bright, owner of Fine Things in Arab, Alabama, has become one of the "fine things" in all three of our lives. Jacob is beloved by not only us, but everyone who is lucky enough to cross his path. We love you Jacob!

ASIAGO CORN PUDDING

6 ears fresh corn, shucked and silked

6 large eggs

1 ½ cups milk

1 ½ cups heavy cream

2 teaspoons salt

1 bunch scallions, minced

3 tablespoons unsalted butter, melted

½ cup shredded Asiago cheese

Preheat oven to 350 degrees. Thoroughly butter a 2-quart casserole dish and set aside.

Using a sharp knife, cut kernels of corn from the cobs into a mixing bowl. Scrape cobs with the edge of a spoon to release liquids into bowl. There should be about three cups of corn.

In a separate bowl, beat eggs until smooth. Add milk, cream, salt, scallions and melted butter and stir lightly. Stir in reserved corn and mix until well blended. Pour mixture into prepared dish and bake for 55 to 60 minutes or until the center is just firm.

Sprinkle cheese over top of pudding in the last 15 minutes of baking. Cover dish loosely with foil if it begins to brown too quickly. Serve warm.

Yield: 6 to 8 servings

BETTY'S *Best!* If fresh corn is not in season or not available, frozen small corn kernels may be substituted.

COLLARD GREENS WITH BLACK-EYED PEAS

2 ½   cups chicken broth, divided

3   jalapeño peppers, seeded and finely minced

1   small Spanish onion, halved

Salt and pepper to taste

2 ½   pounds collard greens, ribs discarded and leaves chopped

1   (15-ounce) can black-eyed peas, drained and rinsed

2   tablespoons white wine vinegar

In a large saucepan or stockpot, combine 1 ½ cups of the broth, peppers, onion and a generous pinch of salt and pepper and bring to a boil. Add collards in large handfuls, allowing each batch to wilt slightly before adding the next.

Cook over moderate heat, covered, stirring occasionally until collards are just tender, about 25 minutes. Uncover and cook, stirring occasionally, until broth is slightly reduced, about seven minutes; discard onion.

Meanwhile, in a small saucepan, combine peas with remaining cup of broth and bring to a boil. Simmer over moderate heat for eight minutes; season with salt and pepper. Using a slotted spoon, add peas to collards. Reserve broth from peas for another use. Add vinegar to greens and adjust seasonings as needed.

Yield: 6 servings

 SISTER *Says!* The cooked collard greens and black-eyed peas in their broth may be refrigerated separately for up to two days. Reheat both dishes gently before continuing with the recipe.

SISTER'S BROCCOLI CORNBREAD

4   large eggs, lightly beaten

1   (10-ounce) package frozen chopped broccoli, thawed

1   small onion, finely chopped

1   green onion, finely chopped

1   cup small-curd cottage cheese

½   cup unsalted butter, melted

1 ½   cups self-rising cornmeal

1   teaspoon sugar

Preheat oven to 350 degrees. Lightly butter a 9×13×2-inch casserole and set aside.

Combine eggs, broccoli, onions, cottage cheese and butter in a large mixing bowl. Add cornmeal and sugar, stirring until dry ingredients are moistened. Do not beat.

Pour batter into prepared baking dish. Bake for 40 to 45 minutes or until cornbread is golden brown and top is firmly set. Delicious!

Yield: 8 servings

FREE-FORM FRENCH APPLE TART

Tart Dough

1 ¼ cups unbleached all-purpose flour

2 tablespoons sugar

¼ teaspoon salt

6 tablespoons cold unsalted butter, cut into ½-inch cubes

4 ounces cold cream cheese, cut into ½-inch cubes

2 teaspoons lemon juice

1 to 2 tablespoons ice water

Combine flour, sugar and salt in the bowl of a food processor. Process for several seconds. Add butter and cream cheese; pulse until mixture is sandy, with small curds. Turn mixture into medium bowl. Sprinkle lemon juice and one tablespoon ice water over mixture. With a fork, use folding motion to incorporate liquid into flour mixture. Turn dough onto a clean, dry work surface; gently press together into a ball, then flatten into a rough disc. Refrigerate until firm, about 30 minutes. Remove dough from refrigerator and roll into a circle. Place circle on a parchment-lined baking pan.

. . . .

Apple Filling

1 ¼ pounds Granny Smith apples (about 3 medium)

1 ¼ pounds McIntosh apples (about 3 medium)

2 tablespoons lemon juice

¼ cup plus 2 tablespoons sugar

¼ teaspoon ground cinnamon

2 large egg whites, lightly beaten

Heat oven to 400 degrees. Peel, core and cut apples into ¼-inch-thick slices and toss with lemon juice, ¼ cup sugar and cinnamon. Arrange apple slices in circle over dough, leaving a 1-inch perimeter of dough for a fluted edge. Fill center with additional slices. Fold outer lip of dough snugly inward over apples and cup with hand to compress and shape.

Bake tart until pale golden brown, about 15 minutes. Brush crust with beaten egg whites and sprinkle apples with remaining two tablespoons sugar. Return tart to oven and continue baking until crust is deep golden brown and apples are tender, about 20 minutes longer. Cool tart on baking sheet for five minutes. Remove from parchment and transfer to wire rack. Cool additional five minutes and serve with vanilla ice cream.

BETTY'S *Best!*

There is no single perfect apple for a pie — it's just a matter of preference. Some cooks favor tart apples over sweet ones. Or a soft-textured pie over one with distinct, firm pieces. (There are traditionalists who only use the McIntosh, which tends to disintegrate when cooked, whereas many prefer the mildly sweet Golden Delicious— the classic choice for tarte Tatin — because it holds its shape.) Tart, firm candidates for pie include Braeburn, Granny Smith, Northern Spy, Cortland, Newtown Pippin, Gravenstein, Greening, Winesap, Idared, Matsu (also known as Crispin), Jonathan, and Jonagold.

Celebrations for Every Day

Brunch
FOR A BUNCH

You know how we feel about brunch: short and sweet, and easy on the kitchen! Not to mention, more time to spend with your guests and more fun for everyone. The timing is great too, as the mid-morning gathering leaves the balance of the day open for sporting events, family time, gardening, or whatever the day brings. And when your friends ask for these crowd-pleasing recipes, just point them to the bookstore for their own copy!

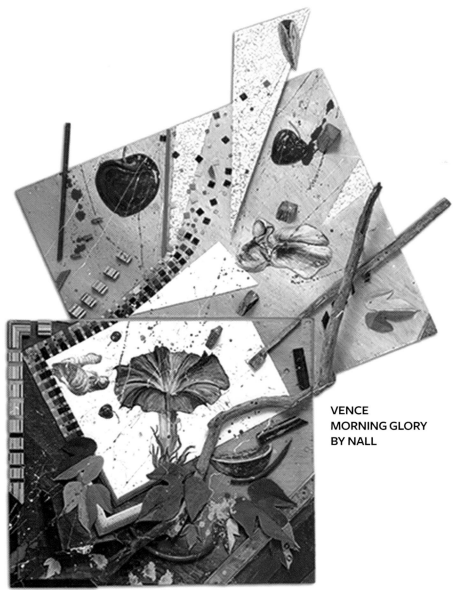

**VENCE
MORNING GLORY
BY NALL**

KIR ROYALES

⅓   cup crème de cassis

2   (750-ml) bottles Champagne, well
      chilled

Chill eight Champagne flutes in the freezer for about 15 minutes.

Remove from freezer and spoon one or two teaspoons crème de cassis into
each flute. Slowly fill flutes with Champagne. Serve immediately.

Yield: 8 cocktails

BETTY'S Best! For best results, look for a high quality crème de cassis (black currant liqueur). The best ones come from the Dijon region of France and produce a refreshing Burgundian-style cocktail.

MARINATED SPICED FRUIT

- 1 (20-ounce) can pineapple chunks
- 1 (16-ounce) can sliced peaches
- 1 (20-ounce) can sliced pears
- 1 cup sugar
- ½ cup plus 1 tablespoon white vinegar
- 1 (3-ounce) package cherry gelatin
- 3 cinnamon sticks
- 5 whole cloves

Drain pineapple, reserving ¾ cup of juice. Drain peaches and pears, reserving ½ cup of the juice. Combine pineapple, peaches and pears in a large bowl and mix gently. In a medium saucepan, combine the reserved juices with sugar, vinegar, gelatin, cinnamon sticks and cloves. Simmer mixture for 30 minutes, stirring occasionally. Pour over fruit, tossing carefully to mix.

Chill, covered, for 24 hours, stirring occasionally. When ready to serve, remove cinnamon sticks and cloves and discard.

Yield: 10 servings

This salad does not congeal, but the gelatin helps thicken the mixture and gives it a pleasing red color. You may also want to use fresh fruit when in season, substituting a simple syrup for the liquid from the drained fruit.

CHEESE BISCUITS

- 1 (16-ounce) block sharp Cheddar cheese, shredded
- 1 cup corn oil margarine
- 1 cup unsalted butter, softened
- 4 cups all-purpose flour
- 1 tablespoon sugar
- ¾ teaspoon cayenne pepper
- ½ teaspoon baking powder
- ¼ teaspoon salt

Pecan halves, at room temperature

In a large mixing bowl, beat together cheese, margarine and butter until well blended. Sift flour, sugar, cayenne pepper, baking powder and salt together in a separate bowl. Add to cheese mixture and blend.

Divide mixture into four equal sections and, using floured hands, roll each into a long log. Wrap in wax paper and refrigerate or freeze for later use.

When ready to serve, preheat oven to 350 degrees. Cut logs into ¼-inch slices and place on an ungreased baking sheet. Press pecan half into each biscuit. Bake for about 18 minutes or until lightly browned.

If desired, serve with a dollop of mint or pepper jelly on top.

Cheese Biscuits make a great passed appetizer to serve as your guests are arriving. Can be made up to 3 weeks ahead and frozen.

SISTER'S ANGEL BISCUITS

1   package active dry yeast

¼   cup warm water
     (105 to 115 degrees F)

¾   cup warm buttermilk
     (105 to 115 degrees F)

2 ½ cups all-purpose flour

½   teaspoon baking powder

½   teaspoon baking soda

½   teaspoon salt

2   tablespoons sugar

½   cup shortening

Combine yeast and warm water in a 2-cup liquid measuring cup; let stand for five minutes. Add warm buttermilk and stir well.

In a large bowl, combine flour, baking powder, soda, salt and sugar. Cut in shortening with a pastry blender until mixture resembles coarse meal. Add yeast mixture, stirring with a fork just until dry ingredients are moistened.

Turn dough out onto a lightly floured surface and knead 10 to 15 times or until dough is smooth and no longer sticky. Roll dough to ¾-inch thickness and cut with a floured 2-inch biscuit cutter. Place biscuits 1 inch apart, 3 to a row, on a large ungreased baking sheet and cover with a damp tea towel. Let rise in a warm place (85 degrees), free from drafts, for 30 to 45 minutes or until doubled in bulk.

Preheat oven to 400 degrees. Bake biscuits, uncovered, for 15 minutes or until tops are golden.

Yield: 1 dozen biscuits

SISTER *Says!* We call these angel biscuits because they are made with yeast, which makes them so light and fluffy they almost fly off the plate!

PARTY CHICKEN, SHRIMP AND ARTICHOKE SUPREME OVER RICE

8   whole chicken breasts, cooked and cut into large cubes

2   pounds peeled, cooked shrimp

3   (14-ounce) cans plain artichoke hearts, quartered

3   pounds fresh mushrooms, sautéed in butter

6   cups Medium White Sauce or béchamel sauce

2   tablespoons Worcestershire sauce

1   cup sherry or white wine

1   cup freshly grated Parmigiano-Reggiano cheese

Grease two 3-quart (9×13-inch) casserole or baking dishes. Divide chicken, shrimp, artichokes and mushrooms equally among the two dishes.

Prepare white sauce as directed below and stir in Worcestershire and wine. Pour over meat, shrimp and artichokes and top each casserole with ½ cup of the cheese. Dishes may be prepared up to this point a day before serving. Cover and refrigerate.

When ready to serve, remove from refrigerator an hour before baking and bring to room temperature. Bake uncovered in a preheated 375-degree oven for about 30 minutes or until mixture is bubbly and hot through.

Serve over hot basmati or regular white rice.

Yield: 18 to 20 servings

NOTE: You may substitute four pounds of shrimp in the shell for the two pounds of prepared shrimp. Boil as usual and shell before adding to the dish.

MEDIUM WHITE SAUCE

1   cup unsalted butter

1   cup all-purpose flour

6   cups whole milk (or 3 cups milk and 3 cups half-and-half)

1   tablespoon salt

1   teaspoon white pepper

Melt butter in a heavy-bottomed large saucepan over medium heat and cook until bubbly. Slowly whisk in flour and stir until well blended, but not browned. Add milk gradually, whisking constantly until thickened. Add salt and pepper and blend again.

Yield: 6 cups

NOTE: And just so you know, if you are making a French recipe that calls for béchamel sauce…well, it is the same thing as the Medium White Sauce called for in this dish. Bon appétit!

ORANGE-CHOCOLATE MOUSSE

1½ pounds semisweet chocolate

4 egg yolks

½ cup brewed coffee or espresso

½ cup orange-flavored liqueur
(Grand Marnier)

2 cups heavy cream, chilled,
divided

¼ cup sugar

8 egg whites

Salt

½ teaspoon vanilla extract

Melt chocolate in a 2-quart glass measuring cup in the microwave at half power for two minutes; stir and microwave again for 2 additional minutes. Add egg yolks, one at a time, whisking well after each addition. Add coffee, and then stir in orange liqueur. Let mixture cool to room temperature.

In a medium mixing bowl, beat one cup cream until thickened. Gradually beat in sugar, beating until stiff. In a separate bowl, beat egg whites with a pinch of salt until stiff. Gently fold egg white mixture into cream. Stir about one third of the cream and egg white mixture into the chocolate and blend. Scrape the remaining cream and egg mixture over the lightened chocolate and fold together well. Spoon into eight individual dessert cups or into one large serving bowl. Refrigerate for two hours or until set.

At serving time, whip remaining cup of cream until thickened; add vanilla and whip until soft peaks form. Top each portion of the mousse with a dollop of whipped cream.

Yield: 8 to 10 servings

Hope is a good breakfast.

ANONYMOUS

More Formal Celebrations

LET'S HAVE A
Cocktail Party!

Hospitality, a synonym for the South, comes from the heart. Hospitality is a gift: it is the giving of oneself, the opening of one's home to create a warm and welcoming spot. If the party is well planned and runs smoothly, everyone has fun, even the hostess.

Engagement? Anniversary? Graduation? Retirement? Just feel like throwing a party?

Whatever the reason, when a big celebration is called for, here is a menu which can accommodate any number of guests. If you want to enjoy your party, we recommend that you hire several servers and a bartender for every 50 guests. Make sure that servers know how you want the food plated for presentation, and check periodically to make sure the kitchen is running smoothly.

Planning, organization, and flexibility are the keys to success for a large party. Seasonal flowers, creative decorations, and plenty of good food and drink will ensure that your celebration is a truly memorable event.

MENU

Cheese Poppers

Warm Shrimp and Artichokes
with Toast Points

Bette Davis Eyes

Sweet Potato Biscuits
with Pork Tenderloin

Tiny Potatoes with
Bacon and Avocado

Oven-Roasted Seasonal
Vegetables with Spicy White Dip

Chocolate Cordial Cups Filled
with Betty's Lemon Curd

WINE SUGGESTION:
Red and White Burgundy
(French Bourgogne)

WARM SHRIMP AND ARTICHOKES WITH TOAST POINTS

1 ¼ cups butter, divided

1 pound mushrooms, sliced

1 ½ pounds shrimp, peeled and deveined

2 (14-ounce) cans artichoke hearts

1 cup all-purpose flour

4 cups milk

¼ cup sherry

1 tablespoon Worcestershire sauce

Salt and pepper to taste

1 ½ cups grated Parmesan

Melt ¼ cup butter in a small skillet and sauté mushrooms. Peel and devein shrimp; cut each in half. Drain artichokes and chop. Set aside mushrooms, shrimp and artichokes.

In a large skillet, melt remaining 1 cup butter over medium-high heat until bubbly. Slowly add flour and stir quickly with a wire whisk to incorporate. Continue stirring rapidly and add milk. Allow mixture to thicken, stirring constantly. Lower heat to medium and add wine, seasonings and cheese.

Stir in reserved shrimp, mushrooms and artichokes and continue heating gently. Transfer mixture to a chafing dish and serve with Toast Points.

Toast Points

1 loaf white bread

Preheat oven to 300 degrees.

Remove crusts from white bread and cut each piece into four triangles, allowing at least 2 points per invited guest.

Place triangles on baking sheets and cook for about 30 minutes. Do not allow bread to brown.

Yield: 50 servings

BETTE DAVIS EYES

4 tablespoons heavy cream

1 (16-ounce) package goat cheese, at room temperature

1½ pounds dark seedless grapes

2 cups pistachio nuts, very finely chopped

Lettuce leaves

Mix cream and goat cheese together until somewhat smooth. Wrap goat cheese mixture around each grape and roll in chopped nuts. Place on a baking sheet and chill. When ready to serve, cut each grape in half and arrange on a decorative platter lined with lettuce leaves.

Yield: 25 cocktail servings

BETTY'S *Best!* Chop pistachio nuts in a food processor. If they are not very finely chopped, the grapes are more difficult to slice.

CHEESE POPPERS

½ cup unsalted butter, softened

2 cups grated extra-sharp Cheddar cheese

1½ cups all-purpose flour

¼ teaspoon salt

½ teaspoon paprika

1 teaspoon cayenne pepper

1 medium jar small stuffed green olives, drained

Preheat oven to 400 degrees.

In a large mixing bowl, blend butter and cheese. Sift in flour, salt, paprika and cayenne; mix well. Pinch a small amount of dough and carefully wrap it around an olive, covering the surface completely. Repeat with remaining olives. Place poppers on an ungreased cookie sheet and bake for 12 to 15 minutes. Serve hot.

Yield: about 80 poppers

NOTE: This hors d'oeuvre, adapted from Noel Shinn's recipe in *Cotton Country Cooking*, is perfect to pass as guests arrive at your party and may even be made ahead of time. Uncooked, they freeze beautifully. Freeze on a cookie sheet to avoid their sticking together. When frozen, poppers may be stored in a ziptop freezer bag. When ready to bake, allow them to thaw on a cookie sheet and follow baking directions above.

TINY POTATOES WITH BACON AND AVOCADO

12	tiny red potatoes
1	pound bacon, cut into 1-inch pieces
1	cup sour cream
¼	cup chopped cilantro
1	avocado, finely chopped
1	large tomato, finely chopped

Preheat oven to 425 degrees. Scrub potatoes and pierce in several places with a fork or knife. Place on a baking sheet and roast for 40 minutes or until tender when tested with a fork. Let stand until cool enough to handle. Cut potatoes in half and scoop out centers with a teaspoon or melon baller, leaving a ¼-inch shell. Set aside. Reserve scooped out centers for a later use.

Cook bacon in a large skillet until crisp. Remove with a slotted spoon and drain well on paper towels.

Combine bacon, sour cream, cilantro, avocado and tomato in a mixing bowl and blend well. Fill reserved potato shells with bacon mixture, slightly rounding the tops.

Serve warm or at room temperature.

Yield: 24 cocktail servings

SWEET POTATO BISCUITS

2 to 3 medium sweet potatoes, peeled
and cut into 1-inch cubes

½ cup unsalted butter,
softened

½ cup sugar

1 teaspoon salt

3 ½ to 4 cups all-purpose flour

4 ½ teaspoons baking powder

1 ½ teaspoon ground cinnamon

Add sweet potatoes to a saucepan and cover with water. Boil until tender when pierced with a fork; drain well. When cool enough to handle, remove skins and mash.

Measure 1 ½ cups of the mashed potatoes into a large mixing bowl and reserve any remaining for another use. Add butter, sugar and salt to potatoes and mix well.

Sift together 3 ½ cups flour, baking powder and cinnamon. Add to potato mixture and mix well. Knead the mixture, adding remaining flour, if necessary, to make a soft dough. Wrap dough in plastic wrap and chill for at least 30 minutes.

Preheat oven to 350 degrees. Grease a baking sheet and set aside. Roll dough into ½-inch thickness and cut rounds using a 2 ½-inch biscuit cutter. Place biscuits about 2 inches apart on prepared baking sheet and cook for 15 minutes or until they begin to brown nicely.

Biscuits may be prepared ahead and frozen for later use.

Yield: 3 dozen biscuits

PORK TENDERLOIN

2 to 3 pounds pork tenderloin

1 cup sweet mustard

Caper Mustard Sauce (page 70)

Preheat oven to 325 degrees.

Remove tenderloins from packaging. Rinse tenderloins with cold water and pat dry with paper towels. Place them on a pan lined with foil and cook for 30 minutes. Remove tenderloins from oven and spread them with sweet mustard before returning to the oven for an additional 30 minutes of roasting. Meat should reach an internal temperature of 160 degrees when tested with a meat thermometer.

Tent tenderloins with foil and allow to rest (and continue cooking) for about 10 minutes before slicing them diagonally. Serve on Sweet Potato Biscuits that have been split and spread with Caper Mustard Sauce.

OVEN-ROASTED SEASONAL VEGETABLES
WITH SPICY WHITE DIP

1	cup olive oil
6	cloves garlic, finely chopped
2	tablespoons fresh rosemary, minced
2	tablespoons fresh thyme leaves, minced
½	teaspoon coarsely ground black pepper
½	teaspoon salt
2	zucchini squash, trimmed and quartered lengthwise
2	yellow squash, trimmed and quartered lengthwise
8	ounces green beans, trimmed
8	ounces asparagus, trimmed
2	sweet potatoes, peeled and cut into thick slices
5	red bliss potatoes, quartered

Preheat oven to 375 degrees. In a small bowl, combine oil, garlic, rosemary, thyme, pepper and salt. Combine all vegetables in a large bowl and add olive oil mixture. Stir to coat vegetables evenly. Place all vegetables except potatoes on a rimmed baking pan; place potatoes on a separate pan. Roast vegetables 20 to 25 minutes or until tender. Potatoes will need to remain in oven an additional 15 minutes. Serve warm or at room temperature with Spicy White Dip.

Yield: 8 servings

 This dish can change depending on the season and availability of your favorite vegetables.

Spicy White Dip

2	cups sour cream
⅔	cup mayonnaise
½	cup chopped scallions
3	tablespoons plus 1 teaspoon capers, drained
4	teaspoons fresh tarragon
2	teaspoons sugar
2	teaspoons fresh thyme leaves
1	teaspoon garlic salt
1 ½	teaspoons freshly ground black pepper

In the bowl of a food processor, combine all ingredients and pulse for 1 minute. Serve with Oven-Roasted Seasonal Vegetables.

Yield: 30 servings

CHOCOLATE CORDIAL CUPS FILLED WITH BETTY'S LEMON CURD

Betty's Lemon Curd

1	cup unsalted butter
3	cups sugar
8	eggs, lightly beaten
	Juice of 6 lemons
3	teaspoons grated lemon zest

Microwave butter on high in a 2-quart glass cup until just melted, about 1 ½ minutes. Add sugar, eggs, lemon juice and lemon zest. Whisk until well combined.

Microwave on high for three minutes and whisk. Microwave on medium high for three minutes longer or until mixture begins to thicken. Continue to microwave on half power until reaching desired thickness. Whisk and cool. The curd will continue to thicken as it cools so don't over cook.

Cover with plastic wrap and refrigerate. Will keep in refrigerator for three weeks.

Yield: 6 cups

BETTY'S Best!

For easier preparation, a bottle of frozen Minute Maid lemon juice may be used, as it is the equivalent of six lemons. Find it with the frozen juice concentrates in the grocery. This is not the same product as the reconstituted lemon juice in the green container!

TIP: If you can't find cordial cups at your local market or specialty store, they may be ordered online at a variety of sites.

Cordial Cups with Lemon Curd

Place cordial cups on a cake stand. Using a teaspoon, fill each cup with curd. Top with a fresh raspberry, mint leaf or whipped cream.

"Bill, my husband, in between making rounds at both hospitals, would come in the back door of Johnston Street Café, my tea room, and say 'Do you have any of that lemon "crud" I can have for my lunch?' (knowing full well that we did). It may not have been the healthiest lunch but when he was in a rush it was an easy, quick, and divine meal for him."

More Formal Celebrations

Elegant Dinner Party
FOR EIGHT

Soft candlelight, quiet jazz playing in the background, and the enticing aroma of Baked Goat Cheese floating toward the front door as your guests arrive for a friendly evening of fellowship, delicious food, and perfect wine. This is a time to pull out all the stops; silver must be gleaming and placed correctly, your best china and linens displayed on the table, and the right number of glasses placed in the right order. Wear a beautiful dress and tie on a pretty new apron if you must, but dress up by all means! We have designed a wonderful menu for you, and you must design the presentation of the dishes to put your own appealing touch on this memorable evening. Bon appétit!

ROSES, CHERRIES
AND APRICOTS
BY NALL

MENU

Chilled Asparagus Soup

Pear Mesclun Salad with Baked
Goat Cheese and Toasted Almonds

Macadamia Nut-Crusted Sea
Scallops with Mandarin Orange and
Poppy Seed Butter

Rice Pilaf with Grapes and
Dried Cranberries

Boursin Creamed Spinach

Sister's Baguettes (page 14)

Fruit Sorbet with Raspberry Coulis

SUGGESTED WINE:
New Zealand Sauvignon Blanc

CHILLED ASPARAGUS SOUP

4 tablespoons olive oil

2 medium onions, thinly sliced

3 pounds tender asparagus, tough ends removed, cut into ½-inch pieces

Kosher salt and freshly ground black pepper

4 cups low-sodium chicken broth

8 ounces fresh spinach

¼ cup whipping cream

Olive oil for garnish

Heat four tablespoons oil in a large pot over medium-low heat. Add onions and cook, stirring occasionally, until translucent, about eight to ten minutes. Add ½-inch asparagus pieces and season with salt and pepper. Cook until asparagus is tender crisp and bright green, five to six minutes. Remove 6 thin stalks for garnish and reserve. Add broth, increase heat to high and bring mixture to a boil. Reduce heat to medium and simmer until tender, depending on size of asparagus, about eight to ten minutes. Add spinach and cook, stirring occasionally, until wilted, about two minutes. Let mixture cool slightly.

Place a fine-mesh sieve over a large bowl; set aside. Working in batches, purée soup in a blender until very smooth. Strain through prepared sieve. Add whipping cream. Season to taste with salt and pepper. Cover and chill until cold, at least three hours.

When ready to serve, cut tips from reserved asparagus and cut stalks in half crosswise. Thinly slice each stalk lengthwise. Divide asparagus tips and stalk slices among six serving bowls. Ladle chilled soup over asparagus in bowls and drizzle each with a few drops of olive oil before serving.

Yield: 8 servings

 SISTER Says! This soup may be made a day ahead of serving. Keep it well chilled.

PEAR MESCLUN SALAD WITH BAKED GOAT CHEESE AND TOASTED ALMONDS

1 ¼ pounds goat cheese, well chilled

1 cup panko crumbs

¾ cup extra-virgin olive oil

¼ cup lemon juice

1 tablespoon honey

Salt and black pepper to taste

1 ½ pounds mesclun lettuce mix

2 pears, cored and sliced into thin wedges

1 cup sliced almonds, toasted

Preheat oven to 400 degrees. Slice goat cheese into ½-inch slices (a total of 16 slices). Gently coat cheese with panko and place on a parchment- or foil-lined baking sheet. Bake the cheese until lightly browned, about 10 minutes. Allow cheese to cool slightly while assembling the salads.

In a small bowl, whisk together olive oil, lemon juice, honey, salt and pepper. Toss mesclun mix with olive oil mixture. Divide lettuce into eight portions and mound each on an individual serving plate. Top each salad with three to four pear slices, about two tablespoons of almonds and two goat cheese rounds.

Yield: 8 servings

MACADAMIA NUT-CRUSTED SEA SCALLOPS WITH MANDARIN ORANGE AND POPPY SEED BUTTER

Butter Compote

4	ounces unsalted butter, softened
2	ounces frozen orange juice concentrate
4	tablespoons sugar
4	tablespoons poppy seeds

Yellow food coloring

Whip together butter, orange juice concentrate, sugar and poppy seeds. Add a dash of yellow food coloring and blend well. Set aside.

Nut Crust

6	ounces macadamia nuts
4	tablespoons sugar
4	tablespoons poppy seeds

Grated zest of 1 orange

Add all crust ingredients to the bowl of a food processor and pulse until coarsely ground.

Béchamel Sauce

2	cups half-and-half
2	ounces unsalted butter, softened
4	teaspoons all-purpose flour

Salt and white pepper

In a saucepan, heat half-and-half over medium heat. Using your fingers, or a fork, blend softened butter and flour into a paste-like mixture and stir into half-and-half. Add salt and white pepper to taste. Bring mixture to a boil, whisking constantly as sauce thickens. Set aside.

Scallops

40	(20- to 30-count) sea scallops

Preheat oven to 425 degrees. Place scallops on a large baking sheet. Spoon a small amount of Nut Crust mixture on each scallop and flatten slightly. Bake for ten minutes or until crust is browned. Remove from oven and leave scallops on baking sheet to begin assembling the dish.

Assembly

12	ounces Béchamel Sauce
1	(15-ounce) can mandarin orange segments in light syrup, drained

Reheat Béchamel Sauce and add Butter Compote; whisk to combine. To plate, spoon a puddle of sauce in center of the plate. Place five orange segments around lip of plate, evenly spaced. Place a scallop between orange segments and serve.

To serve on a buffet, spoon sauce on a platter and cover with scallops. Garnish with orange segments.

Yield: 10 servings

NOTE: The French term for making a flour and butter roux, as in this recipe, is beurre mainé and it is translated as "kneaded butter." It is used as a thickening agent for many sauces.

BOURSIN CREAMED SPINACH

3   tablespoons unsalted butter, divided

½   cup yellow onion, diced

2   tablespoons all-purpose flour

1   cup whole or 2 percent milk

½   cup heavy cream

1   (5.2-ounce) package Boursin cheese

1   (10-ounce) package frozen chopped
      spinach, thawed and squeezed dry

2   tablespoons grated Parmesan

1   teaspoon minced lemon zest

Salt and white pepper to taste

Cayenne to taste

Nutmeg

⅔   cup coarse fresh bread crumbs

Preheat oven to 425 degrees. Coat a shallow 1-quart baking dish with nonstick spray and set aside.

Melt one tablespoon butter in a medium saucepan over medium heat; sauté onion. Cook until onion is soft, about five minutes. Add flour and stir to coat onion. Cook about one minute. Gradually whisk milk and cream into onion mixture, stirring constantly to prevent lumps. Simmer sauce for one minute. Stir in Boursin a little at a time until melted and smooth. Remove saucepan from heat. Add spinach, Parmesan, lemon zest, salt and pepper.

Transfer spinach mixture to prepared baking dish. Melt remaining two tablespoons butter and combine with crumbs, salt, white pepper and cayenne. Add a pinch of nutmeg and toss ingredients to blend. Top spinach with crumbs, pressing them down to adhere. Place dish on a baking sheet and bake until crumbs are golden and sauce is bubbly, about 20 to 25 minutes.

Yield: 8 servings

NOTE: Once dish is assembled, complete with crumb topping, it may be covered with plastic wrap and chilled to be baked later.

To cook well, one must love and respect food.

CRAIG CLAIBORNE

RICE PILAF WITH GRAPES AND DRIED CRANBERRIES

3   tablespoons butter

1   cup diced red onion

½   cup seedless red grapes, halved

½   cup sweetened dried
    cranberries

2   tablespoons white or regular
    balsamic vinegar

2   (8.5-ounce) packages ready-to-
    serve basmati rice

¾   cup chopped roasted pecans

½   cup loosely packed fresh parsley,
    chopped

½   teaspoon salt

Melt butter in a large skillet over medium-high heat. Add red onion and cook until tender. Stir in grapes, cranberries and vinegar. Add rice, pecans, parsley and salt. Cook, stirring often, until thoroughly heated.

Yield: 8 servings

If you don't use the prepackaged rice, you will need 2 cups of cooked basmati rice. Additionally, whole grain brown and wild rice may be substituted for the basmati; if so, omit additional salt.

FRUIT SORBET WITH RASPBERRY COULIS

1   cup water, divided

1   cup sugar

3   cups fruit purée

4   tablespoons lemon or lime juice

In a medium saucepan, bring ½ cup water and sugar to a simmer and cook until mixture is clear. Continue cooking for two minutes longer or until the consistency of corn syrup. Cool.

Combine fruit purée, lemon or lime juice, remaining ½ cup water and cooled syrup. Place in a blender and purée until smooth. Pour mixture into a 1-quart glass dish and place in freezer until partially frozen. Return to blender and purée once more. Pour back into dish or bowl and freeze for at least two hours or until firm.

Yield: 8 servings

RASPBERRY COULIS

3   cups fresh raspberries

1   cup sugar

1   teaspoon vanilla

Add all ingredients to blender jar and pulse to purée. Spoon over each serving of sorbet.

Yield: 2 cups

More Formal Celebrations

A Tea Party
FOR EVERY OCCASION

Most women can remember their grandmother's attic, where dusty memories of dressing up in faded hats and gloves and high-heeled pumps was part of the fun of putting on a tea party for favorite dolls and stuffies. We wore our mother's pearls, served animal crackers, and poured imaginary tea from tiny teapots. Whatever we did, the stage was set for celebrations later in our lives that would include our own wedding china and silver and our own lovely jewelry. Whether we are five or seventy-five, the words "Tea Party" evoke sweet memories. The occasion may be a birthday party, a reception, a wedding shower, or a baby shower. Both our English and French counterparts enjoy afternoon tea. Our menu is founded on this tradition, and we think we have given it the glory and beauty it deserves.

Our Tea Party features indulgent sweet and savory finger-food and truly divine Champagne Punch, a happy combination that will transport your guests to a gentler time and place.

MENU

Champagne Punch

Apple Berry Tea

Tiny Heart-Shaped Scones with
Mock Devonshire Cream

Fruit Tray with
Amaretto Cream Dip

Brandied Almond Spread

Gougères with
Betty's Chicken Salad

Cucumber Tea Sandwiches

Bacon Parmesan Tassies

Cinnamon Pecan Logs

Chocolate-Dipped Strawberries

BRANDIED ALMOND SPREAD

CHAMPAGNE PUNCH

2   quarts Champagne, chilled

2   quarts apple juice, chilled

2   fifths light rum, chilled

2   tablespoons Angostura bitters, chilled

Ice mold for serving

Combine champagne, apple juice, rum and bitters in a large container. Place an ice ring in a punch bowl and pour punch over it. Ladle into cups to serve.

Yield: 50 servings

Add grape clusters, strawberries, lemon, and orange slices to your ice mold before freezing.

APPLE BERRY TEA

8   tea bags, raspberry or blackberry flavor

2   cups water, just to boiling

2   teaspoons pure honey

4   cups pure apple juice

Place tea bags in just boiled water in appropriate sized pot for amount you are making. Steep for 5 minutes. Squeeze excess tea from bags and discard. Stir in honey and apple juice. Heat to serving temperature, being careful not to boil. Transfer to silver teapot for serving. If yours is a more casual affair, use an insulated server.

Yield: 12 (½-cup) servings

NOTE: This recipe may be doubled or tripled.

BRANDIED ALMOND SPREAD

Brandy

1   cup white raisins

12   ounces cream cheese, softened

1   stick unsalted butter, softened

½   cup sour cream

½   cup sugar

1   envelope unflavored gelatin

¼   cup cold water

1   cup slivered almonds

Grated zest of 2 lemons

Pour brandy over raisins in a small bowl. Marinate for 8 hours or overnight, stirring occasionally. Does not need to be refrigerated. Place cream cheese, butter, sour cream and sugar in bowl of a food processor. Pulse to combine. Dissolve gelatin in cold water in a small bowl sitting over hot water. Combine gelatin mixture with cream cheese mixture. Stir in almonds and lemon zest. Drain raisins well and fold into cream cheese mixture. Pour into a greased or plastic wrap-lined 1-quart mold and chill.

When ready to serve, invert mold onto a serving plate and serve spread with assorted crackers.

TINY HEART-SHAPED SCONES WITH MOCK DEVONSHIRE CREAM

Scones

2 ½ cups all-purpose flour

1 tablespoon baking powder

½ teaspoon salt

¼ cup sugar

½ cup cold unsalted butter, coarsely chopped

⅔ cup heavy cream

Mock Devonshire Cream

Preheat oven to 425.

Mix flour, baking powder, salt and sugar in a processor bowl. Pulse a few seconds and then add cold butter. Process until the mixture resembles meal.

Place mixture in a medium mixing bowl and add cream, stirring with a fork until a soft dough forms. Shape dough into a ball. Knead on a lightly floured surface 10 to 12 times.

Roll dough to a ½-inch thickness and cut scones out with a small heart-shaped cookie cutter. Arrange on an ungreased baking sheet and bake for 12 minutes. Remove to a wire rack to cool. Arrange on a serving platter. Serve with Mock Devonshire Cream and your favorite jam in small crystal bowls.

Yield: 20 small scones

Mock Devonshire Cream

1 cup sour cream

2 tablespoons sugar

Mix sour cream and sugar together in a small bowl. Cover and refrigerate until time to serve.

Yield: 1 cup

If you are cold, tea will warm you.
If you are heated, it will cool you.
If you are depressed, it will cheer you.
If you are excited, it will calm you.

UNKNOWN

GOUGERES WITH BETTY'S CHICKEN SALAD

Gougères

2   cups water

1   cup unsalted butter

½   teaspoon salt

2   cups all-purpose flour

8   eggs

Preheat oven to 375 degrees. Line two baking sheets with parchment paper and set aside.

In a saucepan, bring water and butter to a boil. When butter is melted, remove pan from heat. Stir salt into flour. Add all flour at one time to butter mixture. Use a large metal spoon to beat until well blended.

Return to medium heat and stir rapidly for one minute. Put mixture in food processor. Add four eggs and process for 30 seconds. Add remaining four eggs and process for 60 seconds.

Drop mixture by teaspoonfuls, one inch apart, onto the parchment-lined baking sheets. If preferred, a piping bag may be used.

Bake for 25 minutes, switching pan positions halfway through. Remove from oven and let cool slightly before serving, or turn off heat in oven and let gougères remain in oven, with door ajar, for up to one hour.

Serve hot or cool and fill with savory fillings such as chicken salad or with dessert fillings such as lemon curd or white chocolate mousse.

Yield: 40 to 50 small puffs

BETTY'S CHICKEN SALAD

8   chicken breast halves

1   medium onion

1   rib celery

1   carrot

1   tablespoon salt

3   cups chopped celery

2   cups mayonnaise

¾   teaspoon white pepper

⅛   teaspoon cayenne

Salt to taste

Rinse chicken. Combine chicken, onion, celery, carrot and salt with enough water to cover in a stockpot. Cook for 45 minutes or until chicken is cooked through. Drain, discarding the broth and vegetables. Chop chicken, discarding skin and bones. Broth may be reserved and refrigerated for use in soups or other recipes. It can also be frozen.

Mix chicken, celery, mayonnaise, white pepper, cayenne and salt in a bowl and mix well. Chill, covered, until serving time. Spoon a small amount of mixture into prepared gougères to serve.

Yield: 6 cups

NOTE: Sometime when making this chicken salad, try this addition for variety. Drain and chop two cans of quartered artichoke hearts, stir in a tablespoon of dried tarragon, and mix it with the chicken salad.

CUCUMBER TEA SANDWICHES

2 (8-ounce) packages cream cheese, softened

1 cup peeled, seeded and finely chopped cucumber

½ cup minced green onion

¼ cup chopped fresh dill

2 tablespoons mayonnaise

½ teaspoon salt

½ teaspoon freshly ground black pepper

48 slices white bread

Stir together cream cheese, cucumber, onion, dill, mayonnaise, salt and pepper and mix well.

Spread mixture on one side of 24 bread slices; top with remaining slices. Trim away crusts and cut each sandwich into four triangles with a serrated knife.

Yield: 8 dozen

NOTE: To really make an impressive presentation, spread edges of the sandwiches with a thin layer of mayonnaise and dip edges in finely chopped parsley, dill, watercress or even capers.

ABOUT TEA SANDWICHES

You can make tea sandwiches a day ahead and keep them fresh by first covering them with a barely damp kitchen towel and then wrapping them in plastic wrap. Refrigerate until about an hour before tea time.

When making herb-flavored mayonnaise, start with a small amount of curry powder for color and flavor. Remember, dried herbs are stronger than fresh ones, so use a light hand with seasonings.

Use fresh herbs and edible flowers as garnishes, giving free rein to your artistic abilities. Symmetry and neatness count.

BACON-PARMESAN TASSIES

½ cup unsalted butter, softened

1 (8-ounce) package cream cheese, softened

2 cups all-purpose flour

1 cup half-and-half

2 large eggs

⅛ teaspoon salt

8 bacon slices, cooked and crumbled

1 cup grated Parmesan

¼ cup chopped fresh chives

Beat butter and cream cheese at medium speed with an electric mixer until creamy. Gradually add flour to butter mixture, beating at low speed until blended. Shape mixture into 24 balls and place on a baking sheet. Cover and chill one hour.

Preheat oven to 375 degrees. Place dough balls into cups of lightly greased 24-cup miniature muffin pan. Press dough downward, forming a shell.

Whisk together half-and-half, eggs and salt. Sprinkle bacon into pastry shells; top with one teaspoon cheese. Drizzle half-and-half mixture over cheese and sprinkle chives over the top.

Bake for 25 to 30 minutes or until puffed and golden brown. Remove from pan to a wire rack and cool five minutes. Serve warm.

Yield: 2 dozen

FRUIT TRAY WITH AMARETTO CREAM DIP

2 (8-ounce) packages cream cheese, softened

2 cups confectioners' sugar

¼ cup amaretto

1 teaspoon almond flavoring

½ cup heavy cream

1 cup slivered almonds, toasted

Combine cream cheese, sugar, amaretto, almond flavoring and cream in a mixing bowl. Beat until blended, scraping down the bowl occasionally. Spoon into a serving bowl and sprinkle top with toasted almonds.

Serve with assorted fresh fruit such as pineapple chunks, cantaloupe, grapes and melon chunks.

CINNAMON PECAN LOGS

This is one of the few recipes we have that calls for margarine instead of butter. It works the best for a crisp cookie, and we don't substitute!

1	cup margarine (no substitutions)
1	cup sugar
1	egg yolk
2	cups all-purpose flour
2	teaspoons cinnamon
1	egg white, beaten
1	cup ground pecans

Preheat oven to 350 degrees. Grease a 10×15-inch baking sheet and set aside.

Beat margarine and sugar with an electric mixer until creamy, scraping down the bowl occasionally. Add egg yolk, beating until blended. Stir in a sifted mixture of flour and cinnamon; mix well and spread over the bottom of prepared baking sheet. Brush with egg white and sprinkle with pecans.

Bake for 15 minutes or until light brown. Let stand to cool. Cut into 1×4-inch logs and remove from pan immediately.

Yield: 48 logs

CHOCOLATE-DIPPED STRAWBERRIES

25	fresh ripe strawberries
3	cups chocolate chips
1	tablespoon canola oil

Gently rinse strawberries and place on paper towels to dry. Melt chocolate chips in a 2-quart glass measuring cup at half power for two minutes. Whisk and melt two more minutes at half power or until melted. Add oil and stir to mix well.

Dip strawberries halfway up on the berries and carefully place on cooling racks. Let dry and refrigerate until placed on a platter to serve.

BARNES FAMILY FOUNDATION

From the time I could climb on a kitchen stool and hold a spoon, I have loved cooking and baking. Thankfully I was guided by five generations of wonderful cooks in my family. When I was 12 my grandmother, whom we affectionately called Gommey, taught me how to make her parker house yeast rolls. I took my grandmother's recipe for everlasting rolls and turned it into my calling. I was inspired by Gommey's spirit, her talent, and her confidence in me.

After a brief foray in the catering business I started down the path to Sister Schubert's Homemade Rolls. In 1991 I asked God to help me start my business and I would help him feed the hungry people of the world. In essence I entered into a business partnership with my Lord as I already had a personal relationship with him.

The phenomenal growth of Sister Schubert's Homemade Rolls has taken me from my kitchen to the boardroom in a rather short time. My husband George and I were financially blessed when we sold the stock in our company and we decided then that there was a greater purpose for our financial abundance.

In 2001 we set up the Barnes Family Foundation, a nonprofit charitable organization dedicated to improving the lives of the less fortunate and enhancing others in our community through educational scholarships, historical preservation, and compassion for the needs of children. This current chapter in our lives has been extraordinary.

We believe no one should go hungry. The foundation began by helping local food banks and area shelters in their efforts to help feed the hungry. In an attempt to help our young people become more aware of the world around them, we established an annual scholarship for study abroad. These scholarships enable students to have an experience larger than themselves, which they could not have afforded otherwise. This opportunity also enables them to have a hands-on approach to working with people and cultures other than their own.

Julia Grabko, a student at Troy State University pursuing a degree in International Business, is the recipient of a scholarship from the Barnes Family Foundation.

When I recall the times in my life that I have been inspired to try a new recipe or embark on a new adventure or to step out of my comfort zone, I often

WHEN WE PRAY,
GOD HEARS MORE
THAN WE SAY,
ANSWERS MORE
THAN WE ASK,
GIVES MORE THAN
WE IMAGINE...
IN HIS OWN TIME
AND HIS OWN WAY.

wonder where that inspiration comes from. Now I realize these moments have not been ones of great discovery but rather moments of tiny gifts.

In 2001 a friend asked me to attend a local Rotary Club meeting in Luverne, Alabama, where the guest speaker was a missionary. I never saw myself as an international humanitarian worker, but after listening to the missionary speak about the forgotten children of Ukraine, I became one. The passion, commitment, and urgency in his voice stirred something inside me. His words were the inspiration I needed to act. I listened to that quiet voice inside say "Go, this is your opportunity." I knew I would become involved at some level but I could have never imagined how personal my involvement would become. I knew God led me to that Rotary Club meeting but I also knew there was more I needed

to be doing. I simply asked The Lord to let me know when it was time to do more than financial assistance, and that I would be listening.

A few years later, in 2004, I accompanied that missionary couple to Gorlovka, Ukraine. While spending my days at the abandoned baby center our foundation had helped establish, I saw so many children in need. When I least expected it on one freezing cold day at the baby center, God introduced me to Alexsey, our future son. From the beginning I knew it would be difficult for me to resist these needy babies, but I suddenly and com-

pletely connected with 2-year-old Alexsey. There was something in his blue-green eyes, his smile, his fierce embrace, and his badly clubbed feet that I knew in my heart it was a divine intervention. Fourteen months after meeting him, our family welcomed Alexander

McDavid Barnes, our 5th child, into his new home.

Sasha is the Russian nickname for Alexander. With its safe, warm, and comforting tone, I thought it only fitting to name our new foster care facility Sasha's Home. Through it, we are able to provide temporary and permanent homes for children who have been abandoned or orphaned there in Gorlovka. We have seen that the nurture of a caring family will make all the difference in the lives of these children and their parents that we have been able to help at Sasha's Home.

Progressing from an invitation to a Rotary Club meeting, to a trip to Ukraine, to adopting Alex and then building a foster care home in a faraway land is truly an amazing feat. Completely humbled by the task before me and always with God's help, I continue this journey.

The families of Sasha's Home welcome Sister with a party on one of her visits.

Food, Family, and Faith are the themes that run through my life and my business as well. I will never forget that I began Sister Schubert's Rolls by baking rolls for a fundraiser for my church.

Never believe where you are right now is where you will stay. Pray, have faith, and try to be of service to others. There are opportunities to be of service to others every day and your generosity is deeply needed. I encourage you to search for all the projects, people, and opportunities that cross your path and answer them with your hearts!

The political upheaval in Ukraine has made significant and very sad changes to the stability of Sasha's Home in eastern Ukraine. My heart tells me these precious orphans are in God's will, and I pray always for them to be safely delivered from this tragedy.

Sadly, our Foundation must cease operations in the region until socio-economic stability has been restored. Our foundation will continue our work with all the orphans and abandoned children of the world. Someday I hope to return to Sasha's Home to welcome the children back to the home they knew and loved.

I am truly thankful for my family, my business, my charitable foundation, and all the wonderful friends in my life. I cannot imagine where else God will lead me, but I will keep an open heart and watchful eye toward The Lord. I know I will bake bread, share, and be kind to others, always thanking God for the many gifts he has given me.

Sister Barnes

SIMS FAMILY FOUNDATION

Our Sims Family ALS Research Fund administered by the Community Foundation of Middle Tennessee was established by our son, William Arthur Sims, Jr., the year before he died of ALS, Amyotrophic Lateral Sclerosis, often referred to as Lou Gehrig's Disease. This fund only goes to ALS research. The funds are dispersed to hospitals and research labs performing 'cutting edge' research into the cause and treatment of this disease.

Bill knew when he was diagnosed that death was inevitable. Instead of living with fear, he lived his last days to their fullest, continuing his lifelong desire to help others, friends said. He used his situation to raise awareness about this most cruel and ruthless disease. He did not waste much time with self-pity. Though the disease took away his ability to speak, he used a special computer to communicate and always encourage others "to never give up." That was Bill's motto! Never Give Up!!!

Tara, Bill Jr., Will and Alli

232

The Sims Family from left: Sheri Hofherr, Betty, Libby Patrick, Alex Patrick, Carl Patrick, Lisa Wallace and Bill.

My proceeds from the sale of this cookbook will go to
the Sims Family ALS Research Advised Fund.

The Community Foundation of Middle Tennessee

Sims Family ALS Research Advised Fund

3833 Cleghorn Avenue, #400

Nashville, Tennessee 37215-2519

www.cfmt.org

N.A.L.L. ART ASSOCIATION

In 1986, Nall bought Jean Dubuffet's studio The Cocoon, in Vence, France, and began publishing his line engravings. This led to his acquiring the existing Karolyi Foundation and from this creating the N.A.L.L. (Nature Art & Life League) Art Association. Scholarships are often offered to students recovering from addiction. Located on a three-hectare (seven and one-half-acre) estate in a valley between Vence and Saint-Paul-de-Vence, the N.A.L.L Art Association offers artistic training for college students and provides a cultural life through exhibitions and conferences. The facilities include ten cabins and studios for artists and Nall's studio-museum.

Nall (born 1948, Fred Nall Hollis in Troy, Alabama, USA) earned his degree in art, political science, and psychology from University of Alabama in Tuscaloosa and studied four years at the prestigious Ecole Nationale des Beaux Arts in Paris. He has exhibited his work throughout the U.S., as well as in shows abroad in Gstaad, Switzerland, the National Natural History Museum in Paris, France, National Palace of Guadalajara, and Pemex Tower in Mexico City. His participation in international porcelain fairs includes the Carroussel du Louvre in Paris; Stuttgart, Germany; the Château de Bagatelle in Neuilly; at Podium boutique in Moscow, Russia; and in New York's Arts and Crafts Museum and "Murano Memories" group show.

His signature dinnerware porcelain has been produced by Havilind and Parlon, Royal Limoges, The Tunisian Porcelain Company, and Monaco Porcelain

Nall and Prince Albert, *Japanese Magnolia*, installed in Monaco

Nall and Prince Albert, *Peace Frame*, Monaco 2007

Company. He has had four postage stamps produced by the Principality of Monaco. Nall has created commissioned works, permanent and non, for specific spaces, exhibitions, and figureheads, including the National Arts Club, New York, NY; Cathedral of Saint-Paul de Vence; His Serene Highness Prince Albert II of Monaco; The Tuscany Council for Culture; Puccini Festival Foundation; Miami Dade College, Miami, Florida; Monaco Artist in Residence 2013-2014; Pisa International Airport, Italy; St. Francis Basilica in Assisi, Italy; and St. Augustine Museum. Nall designed the sets and costumes for the Puccini operas *Girl of the Golden West* and *La Rondine*. His monumental *Peace Frame* is permanently installed as the doorway to Pietrasanta, Italy, and Monaco. His monumental *Violata Pax Dove* is permanently installed at Troy University, Alabama, and Miami Dade College. His latest monumental sculpture *Japanese Magnolia* is permanently installed in Monaco. Many international museums, including the Boston Museum of Fine Art and the Bibliothèque Nationale Paris, have his etchings in their permanent collections.

He has been awarded the Mary Ellen LoPresti ARLIS/Southeast Publishing Award for Best Art Book for his creation of *Alabama Art* (Black Belt Press) and has been instrumental in promoting other Alabama artists by curating their works into the RSA Hotels in Alabama. He was awarded a Doctorate Honoris Causa from Troy University, Montgomery, Alabama, and Alabama's Distinguished Artist of the Year award from the Alabama State Council on the Arts.

Numerous hardcover books have been published on his work, including *Technique and Symbol* by Alain Renner, *Alchemy* by Hugues de la Touche, and *Violata Pax*, by Vittorio Sgarbio. Nall lives and works in Fairhope, Alabama, USA, and Vence, France.

artistnall@gmail.com

INDEX

Italic and bold page numbers indicate photograph of the recipe.

INDEX

Italic and bold page numbers indicate photograph of the recipe.

Celebrations FROM THE *Heart*

For more information on scheduling a book signing
for your business or group
and to order *Celebrations from the Heart*, please contact:

Amanda Layton

334-335-2232 Ext. 4119, or

alayton@marzetti.com, or

www.sisterschuberts.com, or

Sister Schubert's® Homemade Rolls
P.O. Drawer 112
50 Industrial Parkway
Luverne, AL. 36049